MINIATURE SCHNAUZER

TAMMY GAGNE

Miniature Schnauzer

Editor: Matthew Haviland
Indexer: Elizabeth Walker
Designer: Angela Stanford
Series Designer: Mary Ann Kahn

TFH Publications®
President/CEO: Glen S. Axelrod
Executive Vice President: Mark E. Johnson
Publisher: Albert Connelly, Jr.
Associate Publisher: Stephanie Fornino

Discovery Communications, Inc. Book Development Team: Marjorie Kaplan, President and General Manager, Animal Planet Media/Nicolas Bonard, GM & SVP, Discovery Studios Group/Robert Marick, VP, North American Licensing/Sue Perez-Jackson, Director, Licensing/Tracy Conner, Manager, Licensing

TFH Publications, Inc.®
One TFH Plaza
Third and Union Avenues
Neptune City, NJ 07753

Printed and bound in China

15 16 17 18 19 20 1 3 5 7 9 8 6 4 2

Library of Congress Cataloging-in-Publication Data
Gagne, Tammy.
  [Miniature schnauzer (2015)]
  Miniature schnauzer / Tammy Gagne.
    pages cm. -- (Animal planet. Dogs 101)
  Includes bibliographical references and index.
  ISBN 978-0-7938-3738-0 (hardcover : alk. paper)
1. Miniature schnauzer. I. Title.
  SF429.M58G343 2015
  636.76--dc23
                              2014039266

This book has been published with the intent to provide accurate and authoritative information in regard to the subject matter within. While every reasonable precaution has been taken in preparation of this book, the author and publisher expressly disclaim responsibility for any errors, omissions, or adverse effects arising from the use or application of the information contained herein. The techniques and suggestions are used at the reader's discretion and are not to be considered a substitute for veterinary care. If you suspect a medical problem consult your veterinarian.

Note: In the interest of concise writing, "he" is used when referring to puppies and dogs unless the text is specifically referring to females or males. "She" is used when referring to people. However, the information contained herein is equally applicable to both sexes.

The Leader In Responsible Animal Care for Over 50 Years!®
www.tfh.com

CONTENTS

ORIGINS OF YOUR
MINIATURE SCHNAUZER

It is easy to see why so many dog fanciers fall in love with the Miniature Schnauzer. This endearing breed offers all the spunk of the larger Standard and Giant Schnauzer but in a more compact package that makes him easier to feed, house, and train than his more massive counterparts. The Miniature Schnauzer not only looks like a distinguished gentleman, but he also takes his role as his owner's companion and protector enormously seriously. When you welcome a Miniature Schnauzer into your home, he will make it his life's work to entertain you, exercise you, and guard you from harm for all his days.

THE DEVELOPMENT OF THE DOG

By studying mitochondrial DNA, scientists have learned that wolves and dogs separated into two distinct species approximately 100,000 years ago. No one knows for certain when dogs began living and working with people, but the oldest graves containing both human and canine bones, which were discovered in Germany, are estimated to be about 14,000 years old. The oldest site of this kind found in the Americas, which was found in Utah, was thought to be about 11,000 years old. This information leaves us with a type of a chicken-or-the-egg question. Did people domesticate dogs, or did dogs evolve from wolves on their own?

However the domestication of dogs began, two things are certain. First, the process took a very long time. It might have started as long as 30,000 years ago. Second, and perhaps much more meaningful, the bonds that were created between people and dogs through domestication have evolved right along with the canine species.

When you welcome a Miniature Schnauzer into your home, he will make it his life's work to entertain you, exercise you, and guard you from harm.

The word "schnauzer" comes from a German word meaning "mustached."

According to the Oxford English Dictionary, the earliest documented use of the phrase "man's best friend" was in 1841. It is no surprise that this phrase was coined around the same time period that people began working to preserve the traits of the distinctively different dogs through the careful development of purebreds. It also seems rather appropriate that that earliest grave of a dog and his presumed owner was found in Germany, where the much-loved Miniature Schnauzer and his larger cousins originated.

EARLY DEVELOPMENT OF THE MINIATURE SCHNAUZER

The Miniature Schnauzer is not unlike the expressive pieces of artwork dating back to the 15th century that share his likeness. From Albrecht Durer's 1492 painting titled *Madonna with Many Animals* to the 17th-century works of Rembrandt, the Miniature Schnauzer is a striking image to behold. He is always portrayed as a faithful companion. The breed's devotion has endured hundreds of years along with its signature look.

The word "schnauzer" comes from a German word meaning "mustached." This etymology is fitting because this German breed's own mustache, along with his expressive eyebrows, gives the breed his signature appearance. The only other breeds that share this distinctively animated pairing of facial features are the Miniature Schnauzer's relatives, the Standard Schnauzer and the Giant Schnauzer.

Although we know that the Miniature Schnauzer originated in Germany, less is known for certain about how the breed developed there. Most experts surmise that it was created by crossing small Standard Schnauzers with Affenpinschers and Poodles. From this point, the smallest offspring to embody the Schnauzer appearance and temperament were likely then bred with each other to create consistency within this new breed.

Miniature Schnauzers were brought to the United States in the early 1920s.

In its early years, the Miniature Schnauzer was used as a stable and cattle dog. Schnauzers possessed a strong protection instinct that the breed retains to this day. They were also adept ratters, although they were never utilized for this purpose to the degree that terrier breeds were.

BREED HISTORY IN GERMANY

However the breed came to be, the Miniature Schnauzer was received with immediate enthusiasm. People were drawn to this new variety of the Schnauzer family just as intensely as it was drawn to them. It became popular in the show ring, as a working dog, and as a general companion.

The first Miniature Schnauzer to be registered in Germany was a black female born in 1888 named Findel. Findel's owner, Herr Max Hartenstein, owned a well-known breeding operation called Plavia Kennels. In addition to Findel, seven other females were registered around this same time. Not all of them looked like the Miniature Schnauzers we know today. Two were black, three were yellow, one was black-and-tan, and one was salt-and-pepper. Although little was documented about these dogs' lineage, it was obvious that wirehaired pinschers, Standard

Schnauzers, and Miniature Pinschers were behind them. It is believed that the Affenpinscher was added to the mix of breeds used for developing the Miniature Schnauzer a bit later.

Interestingly, some fanciers claim that the Pomeranian was used for producing small, black Miniature Schnauzers. While evidence is sparse, these crossings can indeed be traced to an area in Germany called Heilbronn. It also makes a certain amount of sense that a toy breed such as this one could have been used for creating a Schnauzer breed of smaller stature. Being a spitz breed, the Pomeranian would have been an apt choice since his larger relatives were used in the development of the Standard Schnauzer.

Other breeds, such as the Fox Terrier and Scottish Terrier, are also believed to have been used in developing the Miniature Schnauzer. There is no significant evidence of the use of these specific breeds either in the way of paperwork or in ongoing traits. Whenever the Affenpinscher was utilized, on the other hand, its dramatic and lasting effect on the Miniature Schnauzer breed is undeniable. The two breeds share many qualities relating to both body and temperament.

BREED HISTORY IN THE UNITED STATES

In 1923, a man known simply as W. Goff imported the first two Miniature Schnauzers into the United States. This pair, which came from Herr R. Krappatsch, had little effect on the future of the Miniature Schnauzer breed in America, however. Sadly, the male passed away before he sired any offspring, and the female produced only two litters.

A woman by the name of Mrs. Marie E. Lewis, later known as Mrs. Marie E. Slattery, had better luck. She imported four more Miniature Schnauzers from Krappatsch in 1924. Just a year later Slattery's Marienhof Kennels produced the first American-bred Miniature Schnauzer pups. Mrs. Slattery subsequently bred some of the first Miniature Schnauzer champions in the US.

The Miniature Schnauzer breed was nearly as well received in America as it had been in Germany. During the following decade, about 150 additional Miniature Schnauzers were imported. Many present-day champions can trace their pedigrees back to about two dozen of these pioneering members of the breed.

RECOGNITION BY MAJOR CLUBS

The first Miniature Schnauzer was registered with the American Kennel Club (AKC) in 1926. Her name was Borte von Bischofsleben, and she was owned by Mr. Monson Morris. She did not end up producing any champions. Around this time Miniature Schnauzers were known as "wirehaired pinschers" and shown as part of the AKC's Working Group breed class. It wasn't until 1926 that the breed was bestowed the Schnauzer name. For the following year, Miniature and Standard Schnauzers were shown together.

The year 1927 brought several exciting events for the Miniature Schnauzer breed. The Miniature and Standard Schnauzers were separated into two classes according to their sizes at this time. They were also transferred to the Terrier Group this same year. Dogs by the name of Don von Dornbusch and Moses Taylor tied as the first champions of the Miniature Schnauzer breed.

The following year also proved to be rather exciting for Miniature Schnauzer enthusiasts. Ch. Viktor von Dornbusch became the Best of Breed Miniature Schnauzer at the Westminster Kennel Club Dog Show, and Ch. Dolf von Feldschlösschen became the first Miniature Schnauzer to win an AKC group. The breed was attracting more and more attention.

While the Miniature Schnauzer was making history in the American Kennel Club, the AKC was working to combine the Miniature and Standard Schnauzers into a single breed. The most devoted Miniature Schnauzer enthusiasts were against this merger. Their intense desire to preserve the integrity of the two separate varieties inspired the formation of the American Miniature Schnauzer Club in 1933.

It was also in 1933 that the first Miniature Schnauzer was registered with the Canadian Kennel Club (CKC) under the breed name Schnauzer-Pinscher. Canadian fanciers didn't establish a breed club until 1951. It was initially called the

The formation of the American Miniature Schnauzer Club was inspired by the desire to preserve the Miniature Schnauzer's AKC breed recognition.

Many of today's Miniature Schnauzers descended from a German Miniature Schnauzer by the name of Fels von den Goldbachhohe.

Miniature Schnauzer Club of Ontario, but the name was changed to the Miniature Schnauzer of Canada in 1955.

INFLUENTIAL PEOPLE

Mrs. Slattery was undoubtedly one of the most influential people involved with the Miniature Schnauzer breed. Her dogs not only became champions in conformation, but they also reached milestones in other organized activities as well. Her Ch. Mussolini was the first Miniature Schnauzer to compete in obedience. Remarkably, he won his class after having only ten days of training.

Another person who had a lasting impact on the Miniature Schnauzer breed was Anne Paramoure Eskrigge. This devoted breeder was among the first members of the American Miniature Schnauzer Club. Her book, *The Complete Miniature Schnauzer*, was first published in 1935 and is still considered the most thorough and relevant guide to the breed.

MEMORABLE DOGS

An astounding number of Miniature Schnauzers in the US can trace their lineage to a German Miniature Schnauzer by the name of Fels von den Goldbachhohe. This famous Schnauzer's son, Mack von den Goldbachhohe, sired the first American-bred Miniature Schnauzers. Unfortunately, he passed away after producing only a few litters, but his sisters, Lady and Lotte von den Goldbachhohe, produced numerous litters. Their names are seen in numerous pedigrees today.

CHAPTER
2

CHARACTERISTICS OF YOUR MINIATURE SCHNAUZER

The Miniature Schnauzer has been one of the most popular dog breeds for numerous years. If you want to share your life with an intelligent, loving, and playful pet, this charming breed is an ideal choice. Don't let his diminutive size fool you—the Miniature Schnauzer is everything that his larger cousins are, just in a more economical package.

PHYSICAL CHARACTERISTICS

If cuteness is a consideration, you couldn't ask for a more adorable companion. Miniature Schnauzer puppies sport a uniquely disheveled appearance. Even after being groomed, they always look like someone has just tousled their unruly hair. Young adult dogs have a slightly more refined appearance, like a playful schoolboy who has been dressed in his best for picture day—but can't wait until he can romp in the dirt at recess. Even Miniature Schnauzers with a little extra gray in their beards possess similarly devilish good looks.

Miniature Schnauzers possess nearly all the same physical characteristics as Standard and Giant Schnauzers. Their wiry coat enables them to spend time outdoors without being soaked or chilled to the bone by the elements. Their well-muscled legs enable them to jump and play for hours on end. Their bark may sound a bit less intimidating than that of their heftier cousins, but they are no less willing to back it up with their own more compact brawn if anyone poses a threat to their revered masters.

BODY

The Miniature Schnauzer's instantly recognizable profile is the result of a straight backline that gradually declines from the dog's withers toward his tail. His sloping shoulders also play a part in his signature appearance. The look is completed with a cropped tail that is set high and carried erect.

BE AWARE!

In recent years smaller dogs have been bred and marketed as teacup or toy Schnauzers, but these extra-small dogs are not a separate variety. They are undersized Miniature Schnauzers. These so-called specialty dogs are bred from the runts of Miniature Schnauzer litters with little to no regard toward the health of these animals. In some cases their smaller size is caused by genetic problems, which are then passed on to their offspring.

SIZE

The Miniature Schnauzer stands 12 to 14 inches (30.5 to 35.5 cm) tall and weighs between 11 and 20 pounds (5 and 9 kg). A Miniature Schnauzer can be a bit shorter or taller but won't be eligible to compete in dog shows because he won't match the breed standard. Despite the breed's small stature, he is extremely robust. There is nothing delicate about the Miniature Schnauzer.

HEAD AND NECK

The Miniature Schnauzer's rectangular head sports a strong, blunt muzzle and thick whiskers. This "mustache" is a huge part of the breed's distinguished look. The head is supported by a strong, well-arched neck that blends into the dog's shoulders.

EYES

It is the Miniature Schnauzer's eyes and eyebrows that are responsible for his endearing expression. His small, oval-shaped eyes may be dark, but they convey an enormous amount of brightness to the people the dog loves most.

EARS

In the United States a Miniature Schnauzer's ears may be cropped or uncropped. According to the breed standard, cropped ears should end in tips and be nearly identical in appearance and size. Uncropped ears should be V-shaped and fall close to the dog's skull. There is a growing trend among breeders to leave ears uncropped due to the painful nature of the process. Many breeders, owners, and veterinarians assert that ear cropping (and tail docking) is not only unnecessary but also cruel. It is likely that the United States will ultimately follow in the footsteps of many European countries in outlawing these cosmetic surgical procedures.

COAT

The Miniature Schnauzer has a double coat. The outercoat has a wiry texture, and the undercoat is close and softer. The outercoat should be a bit rough to the touch. One of the best qualities of the Miniature Schnauzer's coat is that it hardly sheds any hair at all. This trait makes the breed an ideal choice for people with allergies, but it is very important that owners remove dead hair as new hair grows in. When owners don't remove the dead hair, the dog's coat begins to look overgrown and bushy. Overgrown coats are also more prone to matting. If you plan to show your Miniature Schnauzer in conformation events,

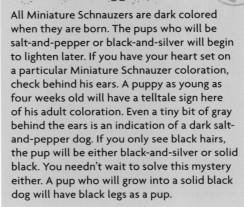

PUPPY POINTER

All Miniature Schnauzers are dark colored when they are born. The pups who will be salt-and-pepper or black-and-silver will begin to lighten later. If you have your heart set on a particular Miniature Schnauzer coloration, check behind his ears. A puppy as young as four weeks old will have a telltale sign here of his adult coloration. Even a tiny bit of gray behind the ears is an indication of a dark salt-and-pepper dog. If you only see black hairs, the pup will be either black-and-silver or solid black. You needn't wait to solve this mystery either. A pup who will grow into a solid black dog will have black legs as a pup.

grooming will be a much more involved task. A show dog's coat must be stripped by hand every three to six months. This technique for removing dead hair takes time to learn and even more time to perform.

COLORS

Miniature Schnauzers come in three different colorations according to the American Kennel Club (AKC) breed standard: salt-and-pepper, black-and-silver, and black. Miniature Schnauzers also come in other colorations, such as solid white and chocolate, but these are not officially recognized by the AKC.

A salt-and-pepper dog's coat consists mostly of black-and-white banded hairs. He may also have solid black-and-white unbanded hairs within his coat, but these are less plentiful in the mix. Salt-and-pepper dogs sometimes have a small amount of tan shading in their topcoats. The hair typically fades to a light gray or silver on certain body parts, such as the eyebrows, leg furnishings, and whiskers.

Black-and-silver Miniature Schnauzers have a coat pattern similar to salt-and-pepper dogs, but in the areas where the former dog is salt-and-pepper, a black-and-silver dog is black.

A black Miniature Schnauzer is fairly self-explanatory, but it is especially important that the topcoat in this coloration is intense black, with softer shades elsewhere. A white patch on the chest—or even an odd white hair anywhere on the body—is relatively common in these dogs.

LIVING WITH YOUR MINIATURE SCHNAUZER

Miniature Schnauzers can make wonderful pets for the right people. Fanciers consider this breed to be everything a small dog should be and more. The breed is not right for everyone, though. If you are sensitive to noise, for instance, the Miniature Schnauzer's tendency toward barking may be an issue. You also may find it difficult to keep up with this breed if you would describe yourself as more sedentary than active. If, however, you are an active person who appreciates the efforts of a vigilant watchdog, the Miniature Schnauzer may be an ideal pet for you.

COMPANIONABILITY

Overall, these tiny dogs adore their owners with an almost unprecedented affection. They want to be with them as much as possible. Unlike certain other breeds that are known for their adoration of humankind in general, Miniature Schnauzers reserve this esteem for their owners, whom they make feel incredibly special.

Fanciers consider the Miniature Schnauzer everything a small dog should be and more.

A Miniature Schnauzer can make a wonderful pet for families with kids, provided the kids are old enough to treat him with respect.

With Children

A Miniature Schnauzer can make a wonderful pet for families with kids, provided the kids are old enough to treat him with respect. It is essential that owners supervise both their children and their Miniature Schnauzers when they spend time together for the safety of all involved. Even the best-behaved dog may snap at kids if they treat him badly. When both children and dogs are taught proper behavior, however, this breed can be a fun addition to an active young family.

With Strangers

Your Miniature Schnauzer will probably never take to strangers as quickly as a Golden Retriever might, but if you make an effort to socialize him, he can become a friendly, well-adjusted dog. Most Miniature Schnauzers are fiercely loyal to their families. Perhaps this is why many owners say that members of this breed make ideal watchdogs. If your Miniature Schnauzer is outside in your yard when a new person approaches your home, he will immediately bark to announce the visitor. Once he sees you welcome this new person as a friend, though, he will warm to her much more quickly.

With Other Pets

Your Miniature Schnauzer will get along well with other dogs, provided that he is exposed to them when he is young. Many members of this breed even like cats. Smaller pets, such as rodents, may be a problem in light of this breed's strong prey drive. Although few Miniature Schnauzers are still used as ratters, the instinct is still alive and well in many dogs. You can train your dog to tolerate small pets, but you should never truly trust him around them.

ENERGY LEVEL

If you visit a litter of Miniature Schnauzer puppies, the first thing you will probably notice about this breed is its amazing energy level. The most laid-back pup in the litter may still be more active than the most energetic puppy in a litter of Bulldogs. Some owners go so far as to call their Miniature Schnauzer puppies hyperactive, and though they will grow into more even-keeled adults, their activity levels will remain high. Even senior Miniature Schnauzers can be surprisingly energetic. If you are used to a dog with lots of get-up-and-go, you should be able to keep up with this breed just fine; but if you prefer a lap-sitter, you might want to keep looking.

ENVIRONMENT

Miniature Schnauzers can live in the city, suburbs, or country comfortably as long they are given adequate opportunity for exercise. For a dog living in an apartment,

Dog Tale

Occasionally, two dogs from the same home are surrendered to an animal shelter or rescue organization. If these animals are especially close, the volunteers may decide that it's best to place them together in a new home. You may find two Miniature Schnauzers who are part of package deal of this kind, or the bonded pair may consist of a Miniature Schnauzer and a different breed.

If you have the time and resources to provide a home for both dogs, I highly recommend opening your home to these animals. You may find that the transition goes especially smoothly because both dogs will have each other's company along the way. As your dogs' new owner, you can feel good about making it possible for these animals to remain together—and about knowing that you rescued not just one dog but two.

this means getting out for at least one brisk walk every day. Ideally, a Miniature Schnauzer should have access to a place where he can run around freely, such as a fenced yard or dog park, on a regular basis.

If you don't provide your Miniature Schnauzer with an outlet for his energy, he will likely release his frustration through negative behavior.

Whereas many breeds need to have one command down pat before learning a new one, Miniature Schnauzers may be ready to move on more quickly.

GENERAL HEALTH

A well-bred Miniature Schnauzer puppy should be very healthy. It is important to bear in mind, though, that every breed is prone to at least a few health issues. A responsible breeder will lessen your dog's chances of developing these health problems by having her dogs tested for genetic diseases and only breeding the healthiest animals. She should also have paperwork to prove her dams and sires have been screened for common hereditary conditions such as hip dysplasia. No matter how thoroughly a breeder tests her dogs or how painstakingly she selects her dams and sires, however, there is no way to predict whether a particular animal will develop a specific disease later in life.

INTELLIGENCE

Miniature Schnauzers are known for their high intelligence. This seemingly positive trait can become a problem if owners aren't careful, however. These dogs love to learn, but if training isn't interesting, they can lose focus. Yes, practice makes perfect, but your Miniature Schnauzer will not want to perform the same command over and over again. Whereas many breeds need to have one command down pat before learning a new one, this breed may be ready to move on more quickly.

PERSONALITY AND TEMPERAMENT

Every Miniature Schnauzer has his own distinct personality. Some pups are more outgoing, whereas others are more reserved. The one you choose may be extremely active, or he might prefer napping on the sofa after a short daily walk. A Miniature Schnauzer can be stubborn or submissive. He can be extreme in his personality, or he may be more moderate.

TRAINABILITY

Miniature Schnauzers typically enjoy training and learn easily. For starters, they are very intelligent dogs capable of learning multiple commands. They also have a strong urge to please their owners, which makes training time more fun for everyone. Owners must make training a priority as soon as they bring their puppies home, however, because these smart little dogs can become rather set in their ways if they are left to "train" themselves.

EXERCISE REQUIREMENTS

One thing you cannot train your Miniature Schnauzer to do is to have less energy. No matter how well you train your pet, he may get into trouble if you don't provide him with sufficient outlets for his energy. This breed needs regular exercise. Without it he may develop a problem with excessive barking, inappropriate chewing, or other forms of disruptive or destructive behavior.

PUPPY POINTER

A Miniature Schnauzer starts to show signs of his personality when he is just a few weeks old. A breeder may even tell you that most pups show signs of their distinctive temperaments almost as soon as they come out of the womb. In nearly every litter, one pup is the most assertive and another is the most laid back. One puppy invariably makes the breeder laugh more than the others. Many but not all of these traits are inherited from one of the parents.

The best Miniature Schnauzer puppy for you may be the one who approaches you first when you visit the breeder. By choosing a pup who readily comes to you from the very beginning, you will stack the odds in your favor when it comes to training your future pet. Chances are good that you will have an easy time socializing this puppy as well, since he is already interested in meeting new people.

SUPPLIES FOR YOUR
MINIATURE SCHNAUZER

Planning your shopping trip will keep you from convincing yourself that your dog needs everything on the market. (No, he doesn't need a piano!)

Have you ever noticed the similarity between the way we react to dogs (especially puppies) and the way we treat human babies? We hold them and kiss them, speak to them in gibberish, and often spoil them with every new accessory and plaything we can find that promises to make caring for them easier.

Dogs are adorable, and spoiling them is half the fun of having them, but it's important to remember your Miniature Schnauzer's age and needs when purchasing supplies. Buying several collars for your new puppy is a waste of money, since he will likely outgrow them before he gets a chance to wear them all. If you provide your dog with a fancy water fountain, he may refuse to drink from a conventional bowl later in life.

Provided you take proper care of him, you are likely to have your Miniature Schnauzer for many years. I recommend focusing your energy on providing him with things he needs to stay happy and healthy. Once he has everything he needs, you can consider buying a few of the superfluous items.

PLANNING YOUR SHOPPING TRIP

It may seem that your Miniature Schnauzer requires an awful lot of stuff for his homecoming day, since he's such a little being. As soon as you start filling the shopping cart, though, you may worry if you've forgotten anything important. Pet supply stores can be overwhelming. You may have never known that you could buy a water fountain with a charcoal filter for a dog, but after seeing one on display, you might worry that you'll be the worst owner in the world if you don't buy this item for your new puppy. (You won't be, trust me.)

For your first shopping trip—and, ideally, for all future ones as well—make a list before you go. Doing so will keep you from convincing yourself that your dog needs every newfangled product on the market. A list will also help keep you from forgetting any of the items that truly do fall under the heading of "most important." In general, your puppy only needs the following items during his first few weeks, and even some of these things are not absolutely necessary.

BED

If your Miniature Schnauzer puppy will be sleeping in his crate, he won't need a separate bed. If not, though, he will. Even if your dog will be sleeping with you, it is wise to provide him with a bed of his own. Dog beds are good for afternoon naps or just lounging on because they're so darn comfy.

Dog beds are available in a full array of shapes and sizes. Which style you choose is mostly a matter of what appeals to you and your dog the most. Whichever bed you select, look for one with a removable cover to make washing it easier. A hidden zipper is also a great feature for a teething puppy.

CLOTHING

A coat is only a necessity if you live in a colder climate and you are bringing your Miniature Schnauzer home during the winter. Housetraining involves spending a lot of time outdoors with your buddy during those first few weeks. Heck, you might want to buy a nice warm coat for yourself while you're out shopping.

Dog Tale

Some owners postpone buying a bed for their puppies until they have passed through both housetraining and the teething phase. This is often a sound strategy. More than one puppy owner has had to buy a second bed when the first one was destroyed. A folded blanket can serve as a temporary bed for your Miniature Schnauzer puppy if you are worried about his destroying a real one.

If you do buy your puppy a coat, I recommend looking for one that is just a little big on him. Doing so might make it unnecessary to buy a second one before next winter because your pup outgrew his first. A dog coat is measured along the back, so you will need to know the length between the base of your puppy's neck and the base of his tail.

If they are made well, dog sweaters can be very warm, but they are often extremely thin and prone to snagging and unraveling, especially in the presence of extra-sharp teeth and toenails. High-performance fleece is a much more durable material for dog coats. Fleece will stand up to the everyday wear and tear your puppy will put it through, and more importantly, it will keep your pet warmer than most store-bought sweaters will. Fleece coats are available in a wide range of colors and patterns. You can even find styles that offer wind-blocking technology.

A coat is only a necessity if you live in a colder climate.

COLLAR

Collars are available in a wide variety of materials and styles. The most durable ones are made of leather, but these are also the most expensive. You may want to wait until your Miniature Schnauzer has reached his full size to invest in a leather collar. The most practical choices are usually made of cotton or nylon. Both are also highly durable and come in a variety of colors and designs. Which one you choose is mostly a matter of personal preference.

No matter which material you select, it is smart to go with a breakaway collar. This feature protects your puppy from becoming strangled should the band catch on an object inside your home. When you take your Miniature Schnauzer for a walk, make sure that you attach his leash to both of the metal loops on the collar to prevent it from coming apart if he pulls.

A collar measurement is taken by wrapping measuring tape gently around a dog's neck. Like the collar itself, the tape should fit snugly, but it mustn't be tight. If you can fit just two fingers beneath your puppy's collar, you know it fits perfectly.

Unlike a coat, a dog collar should never be too big. Most collars are adjustable within a certain range, but you must never use a collar that is still too big at its smallest configuration. Otherwise, you take the chance of it slipping over his head. Should this happen when you are walking your pet, he could run away from you.

HARNESS

Some owners prefer to use harnesses on their dogs instead of collars. A harness can fit more securely than a collar, especially if your Miniature Schnauzer is a wiggler. Harnesses also allow you to pick your puppy up quickly in the event of an emergency—such as an altercation with another dog. (You should never pick a dog up by his collar, as this could injure his neck or throat.)

To take a harness measurement, place the measuring tape around your Miniature Schnauzer's chest, just behind his front legs. The same two-finger rule applies here. Harnesses are indeed safer than collars for some pets, but only when they fit properly.

CRATE

Although crating has its share of critics, many breeders, dog trainers, and veterinarians advocate the use of crates (also known as kennels). Crates make housetraining easier and help keep your pet safe when an outside door must remain open for a while, such as on grocery day. Many dogs cherish their crates and use them voluntarily for everything from napping to enjoying edible treats. Like people, dogs enjoy having a space all their own.

Some people prefer to use harnesses on their dogs instead of collars.

Crates are available in three basic materials: cloth, plastic, and wire. Cloth is impractical for puppies because they can chew right through it. A plastic or wire crate is a better option for several reasons.

Plastic crates are the most popular choices among dog owners largely because of their versatility. They can be set up at home for daily use, serve as a home away from home for your pet when traveling, and break down for easy storage. Although most models include small openings for ventilation, plastic crates typically offer more privacy than wire. This may be a plus when your dog needs a nap or a break from normal household commotion.

Wire crates offer more exposure to household happenings, a plus for an extremely social puppy. Like plastic kennels, wire crates can be used daily and broken down when necessary, but reassembly can be complicated for mechanically challenged folks. Pass up the wire crate if you plan to travel by plane with your dog, though. Airlines only allow the rigid styles, for safety reasons.

An adult Miniature Schnauzer needs a small dog crate—approximately 24 inches (61 cm) in length. This will give him enough room to sit, stand, turn around, and lie down comfortably, but not enough to use one end of the enclosure as a bathroom. Puppy owners should buy an adult-sized crate and block off one end until the puppy gets bigger or is fully housetrained, whichever comes first. A well-placed piece of cardboard usually does the trick, but you can also find dividers made specifically for this purpose.

Finally, don't forget to purchase a padded liner for your dog's crate. This cushion will make the crate more comfortable for your pet. You can find liners made to the exact dimensions of your puppy's kennel in a variety of fabrics and patterns. Some liners offer alternating fabrics, so owners can turn them over to keep their pups warmer in the winter and cooler in the summer. Even if you opt for a liner with dual fabrics, purchase two so that you always have a clean liner when the other one is in the laundry.

PUPPY POINTER

If you have trouble finding a collar small enough for your puppy, try the kitten aisle of the pet supply store. Oftentimes kitten collars are just the right size for a young Miniature Schnauzer pup. No one needs to know that you ventured beyond the puppy section for your puppy's collar. Just be sure you don't choose one with little fish or mice on it if you don't want anyone to discover your little secret.

The bowls you choose can actually affect your Miniature Schnauzer's health.

FOOD AND WATER BOWLS

Your puppy will need fresh water as soon as he arrives home, and he will need to eat soon, as well. You must have a set of clean bowls for this purpose. I recommend purchasing an extra set to help ensure that your pet always has clean dishes.

The most common materials for dog bowls are ceramic, plastic, and stainless steel. Unlike your choice between a leather collar and a nylon one, the dishes you select for your Miniature Schnauzer are much more than a matter of personal preference. The bowls you use can actually affect your puppy's health.

The most obvious risk in buying ceramic dishes is breakage. Drop a ceramic bowl just once and it will shatter. The less apparent yet much more serious risk is lead poisoning. By law, ceramic dinnerware made for people cannot contain lead due to the toxicity of this metal. Unfortunately, no such laws exist to protect the health of pets. If you decide to use ceramic dishes for your dog, skip the pet supply store and head straight to the kitchen department of your favorite home goods retailer. The only way you can be certain your pet's dishes are safe is by buying table-quality pieces.

Plastic dishes won't break if you accidentally drop them. They are also a lot less expensive than bowls made from other materials. However, the tiny crevices that form in plastic bowls over time can hold onto bacteria that can be harmful to your pet. Another concern is the effect the plastic might have on your buddy's skin. In some pets, plastic causes a condition called plastic nasal dermatitis, which causes the skin on their nose and lips to lose its pigment. This contact dermatitis can also be painful.

Your Miniature Schnauzer needs shampoo and toothpaste made for dogs. Human products can make him sick.

The most practical material for your puppy's dishes is stainless steel. These lightweight metal bowls are economical, easy to clean, and nearly impervious to damage from normal wear and tear. Even better, they pose no dangers to health.

GROOMING SUPPLIES

It's unlikely that your Miniature Schnauzer will need a bath the day you bring him home, but it is still smart to pick up basic grooming supplies for him before his homecoming. Your puppy will need a soft-bristled brush, a slicker brush for when he grows up (but keep the soft bristles around for his eyebrows and whiskers), a flea comb, a set of toenail clippers, and a toothbrush. If you plan to trim your puppy's coat instead of hand-stripping it, you will also need a set of clippers. One or two items may need to be replaced at some point, but all of these items should last your pet well into adulthood. Your dog will also need tear-free canine shampoo, ear cleanser, and canine toothpaste.

You don't have to buy expensive grooming supplies, but there is something to be said for purchasing quality items. A metal flea comb is slightly more expensive than a plastic one, but you probably won't ever have to replace the metal one. You won't be doing your dog any favors by spoiling him with human grooming products, though. He needs shampoo and toothpaste made for dogs. Human products can make him sick.

IDENTIFICATION

If your Miniature Schnauzer ever gets lost, your best hope of being reunited with him is a reliable form of identification. Affix your puppy's collar with an engraved tag bearing his name and your contact information. You can order this important item online or create it yourself at a self-serve machine at a local pet supply store. Make sure that you provide your pet with a new tag if you move or if your phone number changes.

Identification tags work well for leading Good Samaritans who may encounter lost dogs to their worried owners, but what if the person who finds your puppy decides to keep him? The biggest shortcoming of ID tags is that they can be removed by dishonest people. This does not mean that a tag is waste of time, but it makes a more permanent form of identification necessary.

The most common form of permanent identification for pets is microchipping. Having your Miniature Schnauzer microchipped is as simple as taking him to the veterinarian for a vaccination. The microchip, which is about the size of a grain of rice, is inserted just under your puppy's skin, typically between his shoulder blades.

If he is brought to an animal shelter, the staff will check him for this form of ID. Both shelters and vets have handheld scanners designed to read these chips, so your pet's identity may also be discovered if another party takes him to a vet for routine care. As with a tag, it is important that you keep your contact information current with the microchip company.

Affix your puppy's collar with an engraved tag bearing his name and your contact information.

LEASH

When buying your Miniature Schnauzer's collar or harness, don't forget to pick up a leash (or "lead"). Even if you have a fenced yard, you'll need a leash for taking your pet on outings and to the veterinarian. Leashes are available in the same materials as collars and harnesses. Look for one that is at least 4 feet (1 m) in length. Many people find 6-foot (2-m) leashes more comfortable, but anything longer than 6 feet (2 m) may be too long for some public places.

You may wonder if you should invest in an extendable leash for your pet. These leashes, which are wound inside hard plastic handles, extend and retract depending on how much freedom you want to give your dog. I have found extendable leashes to be extremely convenient for my own dogs. It is quite literally like having several leashes in one. When walking on the sidewalk, I keep the length closer to that of a conventional leash, but when walking at the beach, I can allow my dogs the freedom to run as far as 20 feet (6 m) ahead of me without putting their safety in jeopardy.

If your Miniature Schnauzer walks nicely on his conventional leash, you may enjoy having an extendable one. If he develops a pulling habit, however, it is better to keep him on a fixed-length leash until you have resolved the problem completely. Dog trainers are divided on the merits of the extendable leash, but most agree that they only make a dog who pulls tug with more might. Regardless of whether you opt for an extendable leash or not, I recommend getting your puppy at least one conventional leash.

TOYS

Every puppy needs three basic types of toys: something to chew, something to chase, and something that can entertain him when he must play alone. Every toy you buy your Miniature Schnauzer will go into his mouth, but at least one of his playthings should be made for chewing. Chewing eases the pain of teething, can

Every toy you buy your Miniature Schnauzer will go into his mouth, but at least one of his playthings should be made for chewing.

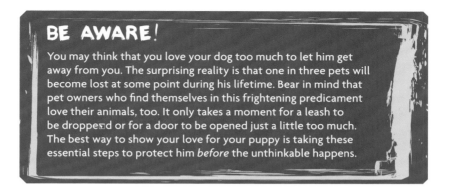

BE AWARE!

You may think that you love your dog too much to let him get away from you. The surprising reality is that one in three pets will become lost at some point during his lifetime. Bear in mind that pet owners who find themselves in this frightening predicament love their animals, too. It only takes a moment for a leash to be dropped or for a door to be opened just a little too much. The best way to show your love for your puppy is taking these essential steps to protect him *before* the unthinkable happens.

help prevent oral disease, and helps keep your pet from setting his sights (and his molars) on your personal possessions.

The list of toys your dog can chase is almost as endless as a new puppy's fountain of energy. Balls, squeaky toys, and flying discs top my list, though. Most dogs tend to gravitate toward one of these popular playthings specifically. The only way to find out which one your dog prefers is to try each one.

Interactive toys are always best, but you should purchase at least one toy that doesn't require human participation. Chew toys may serve this purpose for some dogs, but other dogs need extra stimulation. Hollow toys that owners can fill with edible treats can entertain some pups for hours. Battery-powered balls that roll by themselves or light up for your pet to chase around the room can also be great fun.

When selecting toys for your Miniature Schnauzer, look for items that are small enough for him to carry but not so small that can swallow or choke on them. Toys with tiny pieces that can break off also pose a risk to your Miniature Schnauzer's health. Finally, never give your puppy an item of yours to use as a toy—even if he has already destroyed it. All you will teach him is that he can claim any item of yours he wants by chewing it. For his safety, always supervise your puppy when he is playing with his toys.

FEEDING YOUR
MINIATURE SCHNAUZER

Your Miniature Schnauzer's nutrition is one of the most important aspects of his care. Few things have a greater impact on his health than what he eats. Whether your Miniature Schnauzer competes in an organized activity like rally obedience or gets his best workouts in your backyard playing fetch, his body needs sound nutrition to remain in proper physical condition.

THE BALANCED DIET

Good canine nutrition is about creating exactly the right balance of nutrients for your dog. This important ratio may be a little different for every dog, but each and every nutrient in your Miniature Schnauzer's food plays a role in keeping him healthy. Before you can select the best dog food formula for your Miniature Schnauzer, you must first learn what different nutrients do for his body.

CARBOHYDRATES

Carbohydrates are complex sugars and starches found in certain plant material that serve as an energy source for your Miniature Schnauzer. Because it takes a while to digest carbohydrates, they make your dog feel full for an extended period of time. They also provide him with dietary fiber.

You may have noticed an influx of grain-free dog food formulas on the market in recent years. Does this mean that grains and other carbs should be avoided?

Your Miniature Schnauzer's nutrition is one of the most important aspects of his care.

Because carbohydrates take a while to digest, they make your dog feel full for an extended period of time.

Even the experts disagree about this issue. Many canine nutritionists and veterinarians stake out the middle of the road in the debate, urging dog owners to feed foods that contain moderate amounts of healthy carbs. Many dog foods contain between 30 and 70 percent carbohydrates. Generally speaking, a food that contains between 10 and 30 percent carbohydrates will be healthier for your Miniature Schnauzer than one that contains 70 percent.

The source of the carbs also makes a difference, though. Some of the healthiest carbohydrates for your pet are whole grains— foods such as barley, oats, and wheat. Corn and potatoes are also common carbs found in dog food, but they aren't as nutritious as whole grains. A healthier alternative to a food made from white potatoes is one that includes sweet potatoes, which are also high in beta-carotene.

For some dogs, eating foods that are high in carbs can lead to health problems. These issues may include bloating, constipation, and upset stomach. Consuming too many carbs can also lead to diabetes, increased stool production, and obesity. Carbohydrates, like everything else in your dog's diet, are best in moderation.

FATS

Fats serve two important roles. First, they provide energy. Fats are in fact the most concentrated energy source in your dog's diet. Second, they provide the body with essential fatty acids. Omega-3 and omega-6 fatty acids help maintain healthy skin, strengthen the immune system, and play a role in cell growth.

Ten to fifteen percent of an adult Miniature Schnauzer's diet should be made up of fats. If your pet is extremely active, he may need a bit more, but no dog should eat food that is more than 25 percent fat. The type of fat your dog is eating is also important. The healthiest fats, which contain those omega-3 and omega-6 fatty acids, are found in flaxseed oil, wheat germ oil, salmon, and many other types of fish.

Dogs need a certain amount of fat to survive, but as with any nutrient, too much fat is bad for your Miniature Schnauzer. Consuming too much fat will increase his weight. It will also heighten his risks for a number of health problems, including diabetes, heart disease, and pancreatitis.

MINERALS

When people talk about nutrition, they often group vitamins and minerals together, but there are some important differences between them. Vitamins are organic material, meaning they are found in animals and plants, whereas minerals are inorganic, found in soil and water. Your dog's body is actually capable of manufacturing certain vitamins, but it cannot make minerals. Minerals work in conjunction with vitamins, enzymes, and other minerals to perform such jobs as forming bone and cartilage, maintaining muscles and nerves, and producing hormones.

Minerals must be delivered to your pet in the proper balance. For example, your Miniature Schnauzer can suffer from either too much or too little calcium and phosphorus if these minerals are not provided to your pet in the correct ratio. The best source for all of your dog's nutrients is his food, but this is perhaps most important when it comes to minerals, because feeding supplements can be tricky and dangerous. Your vet can tell you if your dog needs supplementation and how to do so properly.

PROTEINS

If you had to describe one nutrient as the most important one for your pet, it would have to be protein. Protein provides your dog with amino acids that are essential for the growth and repair of body tissue. It also helps the body

Protein provides amino acids that are essential for the growth and repair of body tissue.

produce the antibodies that make up your dog's immune system. Excess protein is eliminated in your dog's urine instead of being stored in the body, so he needs to eat protein every day.

Lean meats are the healthiest source of this vital nutrient. Soybeans are also high in protein, but they lack an important amino acid called taurine. Without taurine, your Miniature Schnauzer can suffer from cardiovascular problems.

VITAMINS

Vitamins can be divided into two sub-categories: fat-soluble and water-soluble. Excess amounts of fat-soluble vitamins (such as A, D, E, and K) are stored within the body, whereas excess water-soluble vitamins (like B-complex vitamins) are excreted through your dog's urine. One might assume that being able to store vitamins within the body is a useful ability, but just because your dog can store vitamins this way doesn't mean that it is always healthy for him to do so. If too much of a particular vitamin builds up in your dog's system over time, it can reach a toxic level.

The chance of your dog accumulating too much of a particular fat-soluble vitamin in his body from his food is unlikely. Supplements, on the other hand, have a greater potential of poisoning your pet if given in excess. For this reason, always check with your doctor before giving him any vitamin supplement.

WATER

Provide your dog with access to plenty of fresh drinking water at all times. Like every other living thing, your Miniature Schnauzer needs water to survive. Water transports all of the other nutrients throughout his body. It also helps regulate his body temperature and allows him to rid his body of wastes.

Dogs eating canned food typically drink less water than those who eat kibble. Other dogs just tend to drink less water than others. If your Miniature Schnauzer doesn't seem to like water, you can help him stay sufficiently hydrated by offering food and snacks with a high water content, such as apples or celery.

WHAT TO FEED

The number of high-quality dog food brands available today is significantly higher than it was about a decade ago. Although this may make deciding what to feed your pet more complicated, the variety of foods dog owners have to choose from is hardly a bad thing. If you have a puppy and the food your breeder was feeding him fits the criteria for a healthy food, it may be best to stick with it. If you think another food may be better, you have plenty of healthy choices available to you.

Provide your dog with plenty of fresh drinking water at all times.

On dog food labels, ingredients must be listed in descending order by weight, so the first ingredient is the most prevalent. Many owners insist that grain-free is the way to go; others feel that providing some carbohydrates benefits growing puppies. What matters most is that the food you select contains more meats than grains, or more protein than carbs. Also, look for foods containing lean meats. You can find healthy formulas made from everything from chicken to venison. Which food is the best for your dog may be completely different from

what's best for another breed or even another Miniature Schnauzer.

Rule out any food that contains by-products or chemical preservatives. By-products are the parts of an animal deemed unfit for human consumption. Chemical preservatives like BHA, BHT, and ethoxyquin give food a longer shelf life, but all three have been shown to cause health problems in dogs. Tocopherols are vitamin-based preservatives that pose no such risks for your dog's well-being.

COMMERCIAL FOODS

Commercial foods, or prepackaged dog foods, have been around for more than a century. A top-quality commercial food is created to meet all your dog's nutritional needs. High-quality dog foods aren't cheap, but by selecting the right one for your pet, you can lower your dog's chances of suffering from numerous health problems and save yourself the cost of related veterinary bills in the process.

Prepackaged foods are available in a wide range of formulas and with a large variety of ingredients. Does your Miniature Schnauzer compete in a sport? You can find a food made specifically for active dogs. Is your Miniature Schnauzer allergic to beef or chicken? How about a food made from bison instead? You can even find a food made especially for a breed the size of your Miniature Schnauzer.

Dry

By far the most popular commercial dog food medium is kibble. It is convenient and economical, and it doesn't spoil quickly. All an owner has to do to serve dry food is open a bag and pour; no preparation is needed. Certainly, you will pay more for a high-quality brand of kibble, but apples to apples, top-quality kibble is less expensive than either semi-moist or canned food. You also won't have to toss a bowl of dry food that has been sitting for more than an hour. Because it is hard and crunchy, kibble is also better for your dog's teeth than wet foods are.

The downside of dry food is that it can be bland, especially for a finicky eater. Some owners think that dry food offers less variety than canned foods because with the latter they can purchase a week's worth of food that includes seven different flavors. Dry doesn't have to be dull, however. Kibble is available in virtually all the same flavors as canned food, and two or more types can be mixed together to add some variety.

Canned

It's easy to understand why most dogs love canned food. In addition to having a more pleasing aroma than dry food, wet food looks (and I suspect it tastes) more like its ingredients than kibble does. Because it is canned, wet food also doesn't need preservatives to keep it fresh like dry food does. Leftover canned food will keep for a short time in the refrigerator as long as you cover it with tinfoil. Be sure that you toss it a few days after you open it, though, as it spoils much more quickly than its dry equivalent.

The biggest drawback to canned food is that it is typically up to 70 percent water. Although your dog will get more protein with most canned foods, he will be getting considerably fewer nutrients per pound (0.5 kg). When you buy

PUPPY POINTER

Puppies have higher protein needs than adult dogs. For this important reason, you should provide your pet with a food made specifically for puppies until he is fully grown. Some Miniature Schnauzer pups reach their adult height and weight by the age of six months; others may take up to a year to fill out completely. If you are in doubt as to whether your dog is done growing, ask your veterinarian.

canned food, you are paying for this high amount of water, making canned food considerably more expensive than kibble.

Another disadvantage to canned fare is the negative effect it can have on your dog's teeth. Wet food morphs into plaque and tartar remarkably quickly. This doesn't have to be a deal breaker as long as you are willing to keep up with brushing. A dog who eats canned food will need his teeth brushed daily. In this case, the timetable is not negotiable—"as often as possible" just isn't enough. You must brush every single day.

Semi-Moist

If your Miniature Schnauzer is a picky eater, a semi-moist food may whet his elusive appetite. Some of the best semi-moist foods are sold in rolls, but always check the label to make sure that the brand you choose is made up of healthy ingredients. Many semi-moist foods contain high amounts of sugar. You wouldn't sprinkle sugar on top of your dog's food every day to get him to eat, right? Don't try to win him over with a food with the sugar on the inside either.

Healthy semi-moist foods are tasty enough to win your dog over without any of the bad stuff. Most dogs find semi-moist foods so tasty, in fact, that some trainers suggest cutting them up and using them as training treats. (If you go this route, however, you can actually diminish the effect of these treats by feeding semi-moist food as the norm.) It's difficult to find a flaw with a top-notch semi-moist food, but if this medium has just one drawback, it has to be the effect the food can have on your dog's teeth. While semi-moist fare won't morph into calculus as quickly as canned grub, your Miniature Schnauzer's teeth will ideally need to be brushed once a day.

NONCOMMERCIAL FOODS

The term "dog food" has become almost synonymous with prepackaged diets, but the truth is that your dog's food is whatever you choose to feed him. It doesn't have to come out of a bag, or a roll, or even a can. Dog food can also be made with fresh ingredients that you prepare yourself.

Home-Cooked Diet

Many of the same lean meats, fresh vegetables, and whole grains that you eat yourself are good for your Miniature Schnauzer as well. By feeding your pet the same food you feed the rest of your family, you know exactly what he is eating. Because the food is fresh, there is no need for preservatives. You can choose the leanest cuts of meats, organic veggies, and just the right amount of the healthiest

Dogs who eat canned food must have their teeth brushed daily.

carbohydrates. Because you will be preparing different meals each day, you can also give your pet something that is much harder to give him with prepackaged dog food: variety.

If you are considering cooking for your Miniature Schnauzer, it is very important that you discuss the endeavor with his veterinarian before beginning. She can help point you in the right direction in terms of menu selection and serving sizes. It is absolutely essential that you learn as much as you can about your dog's nutritional needs when you cook for your pet exclusively.

One of the most important things to remember when cooking for your dog is that he does not need spices in his food to make it appealing. In fact, seasoning your pet's meals can hurt him because some spices contain high amounts of sodium. Mustard and chili powder contain extremely high amounts of sodium, and celery seed, cumin, and saffron contain moderate amounts of this mineral. A dog who consumes too much sodium may suffer from diarrhea, vomiting, and even seizures. For this reason you should avoid feeding your pet high-sodium foods such as bacon and canned vegetables as well.

It is also essential to know which human foods are dangerous for dogs if you will be cooking for your Miniature Schnauzer. Most people know that chocolate is toxic to dogs, but did you know that grapes and onions are also poisonous for your canine pet? While dairy products aren't poisonous, many dogs are lactose intolerant—they lack the ability to properly digest milk-based products. This intolerance often results in diarrhea.

It is essential to understand that home-cooking is not the same thing as feeding your dog table scraps. Your Miniature Schnauzer needs to eat a complete, well-balanced diet created just for him—not whatever is left after the human family members have eaten. When you cook for your pet, you may sometimes need to adjust your recipes, eliminating certain ingredients or making a special batch for your dog without those ingredients. For example, your homemade spaghetti and meatballs may be an extremely healthy dish for your dog as long as you omit the onions and go easy on the garlic.

If you are unsure if you are covering all your pet's nutritional bases, supplement his home-cooked meals with some kibble. Perhaps you can give him a high-quality prepackaged dog food for breakfast each morning and allow him to have what everyone else is having for dinner. You can also add a small amount of kibble to his home-cooked meals. Likewise, if you would like to offer a little variety to a dog who eats kibble on a daily basis, you can do

When you cook for your pet, you sometimes need to adjust your recipes so they're safe for canine consumption.

so by supplementing the kibble with some home-cooked fare.

If you go the home-cooked route, it is extremely important that you make your dog's dental care a top priority. A Miniature Schnauzer eating home-cooked meals will develop plaque and tartar just as quickly as one who eats canned food on a regular basis. Offering your pet crunchy dog biscuits is a great way to add some abrasion to the mix. Raw carrots have a similar effect, but all the biscuits and raw veggies in the world won't take the place of your pet's toothbrush.

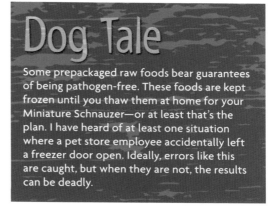

Dog Tale

Some prepackaged raw foods bear guarantees of being pathogen-free. These foods are kept frozen until you thaw them at home for your Miniature Schnauzer—or at least that's the plan. I have heard of at least one situation where a pet store employee accidentally left a freezer door open. Ideally, errors like this are caught, but when they are not, the results can be deadly.

Raw Diet

One feeding program that has become increasingly popular in recent years is the raw diet. Often called the BARF diet, standing for "bones and raw food," this regimen involves feeding uncooked meats and vegetables. Proponents of raw food assert that cooking foods at high temperatures significantly reduces the amounts of certain nutrients within them. The heat and pressure used in the creation of most commercial foods make it necessary for the manufacturers to add vitamins and minerals back into their products before sealing the packages. Raw foods need no such supplementation because they retain all their nutritional content.

Many breeders and owners swear by feeding raw foods, citing their dogs' improved health and overall vigor as proof that this type of plan works well. Raw food followers also point out that eating raw food is what dogs do in the wild. Many veterinarians, however, discourage raw food. While they concede that there are advantages to feeding raw, they see the risks involved as far too great. When a dog succumbs to *E. coli* or *Salmonella*, the condition is usually very serious. Other conditions that vets treat regularly as a result of the BARF diet include choking and intestinal bleeding and blockages from bones.

Some owners feed their dogs raw meat and vegetables from their local grocery stores. Others purchase prepackaged raw food that is formulated specifically for the canine body. You can find several raw food brands at your local pet supply store.

If you want to offer your Miniature Schnauzer some of the benefits of raw food, add fresh vegetables to his regular diet. By doing this, he will get many of the advantages of a raw diet without the risk of illness. Some of the healthiest raw veggies you can feed your dog include broccoli, cauliflower, carrots, and zucchini. The foods will retain most of their nutritional value even if you lightly steam them, and they will be far easier for your pet to digest this way.

BE AWARE!

A Miniature Schnauzer who is approximately one year old should be eating about 1 cup (237 ml) of a quality dog food each day. Be sure to read the label of the food you choose, however, because some foods are denser in calories and nutrients and should therefore be fed in slightly smaller amounts.

BONES AND RAWHIDE

Avoid cooked bones, which can splinter, leaving your pet vulnerable to intestinal blockages and injuries. Rawhide chews may seem like a logical alternative, but they are not regulated by the Food and Drug Administration (FDA) and can contain antibiotics, insecticides, and other dangerous chemicals. Some are even preserved with arsenic. Also, rawhide pieces that break off during chewing can become lodged in your dog's throat or intestinal tract.

WHEN TO FEED YOUR MINIATURE SCHNAUZER

Dogs who eat at the same times each day are easier to housetrain than those who are free-fed, and owners of dogs fed on a schedule are more in tune with their pets' health. They know when their pets have a loss of appetite, a common sign of a health problem. They also know exactly how much their pets are eating because they typically measure servings instead of topping off a dish each day. Free-fed dogs, meaning dogs who are allowed to eat as much as they want whenever they want, are more likely to overeat. This habit leads to obesity over time. Continuing to schedule-feed your Miniature Schnauzer even after he has settled into your home is a smart idea for everyone involved for these reasons.

An eight-week-old Miniature Schnauzer puppy needs to eat at least three times a day. When your puppy is about four months old, you can eliminate his midday meal, but be sure to add the amount of food he would be eating then to his other meals, dividing it evenly between breakfast and dinner. Even though he doesn't need to eat as often, he still needs to consume the same number of calories.

Once your Miniature Schnauzer starts eating adult food, he should be eating twice each day. Divide his daily food portion evenly between these two meals. Feed your pet once in the morning and once in the evening, ideally at the same times the rest of the household gathers for breakfast and dinner. When it comes to your dog's feeding schedule, consistency is very important. Feeding your pet at the same times will help to keep him reliably housetrained. Dogs who eat on schedules also tend to behave better than animals that are fed erratically.

OBESITY

One of the most important things to consider in managing your dog's diet is his weight. Weight plays a role in nearly every aspect of your pet's health. If your adult Miniature Schnauzer weighs between 10 and 15 pounds (4.5 and 7 kg), he is probably getting just the right amount of calories. If your pet doesn't weigh quite as much as he should, he probably isn't getting enough food. More often, though, dogs get too much food and pack on the pounds (kg) gradually as a result.

Feed your Mini Schnauzer on a regular schedule. This will keep him more satisfied and less inclined to beg for table scraps!

Regular exercise and reasonable food portions will help you keep your Miniature Schnauzer's weight within a healthy range.

If an owner doesn't take steps to reduce their animal's weight in this situation, the dog can move from being overweight to being obese, a much more serious problem. Overweight and obese dogs face higher risks of developing cancer, diabetes, heart disease, hip dysplasia, and osteoarthritis. They are even more prone to suffering from certain injuries. The easiest thing you can do to lower your dog's chances of suffering from these problems is to keep his weight in check.

HOW TO DETERMINE OBESITY

A quick way to tell if your Miniature Schnauzer is overweight is to feel his ribs. They shouldn't be prominent, but they should be easily discernible. If you can't feel them without pressing your fingers into his chest too deeply, chances are good that your pet is carrying some extra weight. Whether your dog passes this test or not, it is a good idea to weigh him about once a month. The easiest way to weigh your dog at home is to step onto your bathroom scale with him in your arms. Once you have your combined weight, you can weigh yourself alone and subtract this amount from the previous number. If you notice a sudden increase or decrease in your dog's weight, it could signal a medical issue.

WHAT TO DO

If your dog is already overweight, talk to your veterinarian. Together you can create a sound plan for getting your dog back into shape. If your pet is clinically obese—more than 20 percent above his healthy weight—you will need to begin with diet alone. Exercising an obese pet must be done very carefully to avoid injuries and overexertion, especially if your pet suffers from any illnesses.

Adjust your dog's diet gradually. If you reduce the amount of calories he is consuming too quickly, you can alter his metabolism so that it actually takes him longer to lose the excess weight. Begin by cutting back on your pet's food by about 1/8 cup for every 2 cups you are feeding. You also must cut back on your pet's treats considerably, almost eliminating them entirely. When you do treat your pet, give him fresh veggies in minimal amounts.

Weigh your dog after a week or two of maintaining his new diet. If he hasn't lost any weight, cut down on his food a bit more. Be sure to give this adjustment some time to take effect. Weigh your pet after another week or two. Once he begins losing weight, you know you have found the right amount of food. Continue feeding him servings this size until he has reached his goal.

As your pet begins losing weight, you should be able to increase his activity level gradually. Sometimes health conditions that originally limited a pet's ability to exercise are improved by losing a little weight. Talk to your vet about increasing your dog's exercise as he moves closer to a healthy body size. Regular exercise and reasonable food portions will help you keep his weight within a healthy range.

CHAPTER 5

GROOMING YOUR
MINIATURE SCHNAUZER

Miniature Schnauzers do not need as much coiffing as many other breeds do, but a certain amount of grooming will be necessary to keep your pet looking and feeling good. While styling your Miniature Schnauzer's hair will be a much simpler task if he doesn't compete in the show ring, other grooming tasks have no such shortcuts.

WHY GROOMING IS IMPORTANT

Even if you send your dog out to a professional groomer for the major tasks like baths and haircuts, you will need to perform some basic grooming chores at home between these appointments. Brushing your Miniature Schnauzer every day will keep mats from forming in his coat—and no matter how often you brush your dog or how you care for his coat, he will need regular baths to stay clean. You will also need to trim your dog's nails about once every two or three weeks, depending on how quickly they grow, clean your dog's eyes and ears, and care for the teeth. Continuing to make these important tasks a priority through your Miniature Schnauzer's lifetime will help to keep him happy and healthy.

GROOMING HEALTH CHECK

At-home grooming provides you with the opportunity to stay on top of your Miniature Schnauzer's health. Oftentimes the first signs of an illness can be identified when grooming your pet. Dry or itchy skin may indicate a food allergy or a flea infestation. A red eye can alert you to an injury. Foul-smelling ears may signal an infection.

Continuing to make grooming tasks a priority will help to keep your Miniature Schnauzer happy and healthy.

Dog Tale

You can help your Miniature Schnauzer enjoy grooming more by enjoying it more yourself. Think of grooming as an opportunity to spend some fun time with your pet. Before brushing him, give him a relaxing massage. Play some music while you clip or hand-strip his coat. Buy bright-colored towels for his bath. Finally, don't forget to grab some treats when gathering your dog's grooming supplies. I've developed a habit of singing to my own dogs when I bathe them, but I know that they only tolerate my off-key serenades for the free snacks I provide when I'm done.

Always be on the lookout for anything unusual when grooming your pet, and make an appointment with your vet if you discover something that concerns you.

GROOMING SUPPLIES

Your Miniature Schnauzer should have a set of basic grooming tools, including:
- absorbent bath mat
- canine ear cleanser, preferably without alcohol
- canine shampoo
- canine toothbrush or finger toothbrush
- canine toothpaste
- flea comb
- grooming chalk or grooming powder
- grooming scissors
- hand towel
- large towels (at least two)
- slicker brush
- soft-bristled brush
- toenail clippers
- washcloth

If you plan to strip your dog's coat, you will need a stripping knife as well. In addition to these grooming supplies, you may want to pick up a few additional items to make grooming easier and safer. This short list includes detangling spray (which helps you brush away snarls before they become mats), conditioner (useful for bathing a dog with dry hair or skin—always purchase conditioners made specifically for dogs), cotton balls (useful for many purposes, including ear-cleaning and keeping water out of the ears during bathing), and styptic powder or a styptic pencil (for stopping the bleeding if you accidentally cut the quick on your dog's toenail).

COAT AND SKIN CARE

Begin grooming your Miniature Schnauzer as soon as possible. True, he probably won't arrive home in desperate need of a brushing or shampooing, but getting him accustomed to these important tasks early will make performing them easier on you both later. The longer you wait to expose your dog to being brushed and bathed, the harder these jobs may be when you get around to them.

BRUSHING

Brushing your Miniature Schnauzer prevents mats from forming, removes dirt, dead hair, and other debris from his coat, and releases oils from his skin that are good for the coat. Daily brushings are ideal, but you should perform this important task at least three times a week. For Miniature Schnauzers with shorter pet clips, weekly brushings may be sufficient.

When your Miniature Schnauzer is an adult, you should use a slicker brush on his coat. You will need the wire bristles for getting through both the coarser hair on your dog's body and his softer undercoat. The soft-bristled brush you used on him when he was a puppy, however, will still be useful for grooming his eyebrows and whiskers, so don't get rid of it.

How to Brush

Place your dog in a standing position on a level surface. A grooming table is best, especially for a show coat, but some owners prefer to sit on the floor while brushing their dogs. Never place your dog on a high surface such as a counter or regular table for grooming. A fall from

PUPPY POINTER

Whether you perform all grooming tasks yourself or just the day-to-day stuff, the time you spend on grooming your puppy will strengthen the bond between you. Gentle grooming builds trust. Before your Miniature Schnauzer puppy knows what you are going to do with a brush or a set of nail clippers, these tools may frighten him. Once he learns how good brushing makes him feel and that snipping off the end of his toenail doesn't hurt, he will see that you are doing these things to take care of him.

this height could injure him. You should also never leave your dog unattended while on a grooming table. Safety features like safety loops won't prevent him from jumping if you walk away.

1. Begin brushing by moving the brush in the direction of the fur's growth. Be sure that you are reaching your Miniature Schnauzer's skin, but don't bear down so hard that you hurt him. Many owners find it convenient to start brushing at the head and moving toward the tail. Don't forget to brush the chest, belly, and legs.

2. Next, brush the fur in the opposite direction. Performing this step will help loosen any dead hair or other debris trapped deep within the coat. Again, brush your entire dog—from one end to the other and everything in between.

3. Finally, brush all the hair back in the direction of its growth. If you want to be as thorough as possible, finish off by combing your Miniature Schnauzer to make sure that you didn't miss any tangles.

HAND-STRIPPING

Miniature Schnauzers typically blow their coats, or shed their undercoats, once every two or three months, so you will need to either strip or clip your dog about this often. The more you brush your dog, the easier these tasks will be. Hand-stripping (or "hand-plucking") allows the Miniature Schnauzer's coat to retain its original salt-and-pepper color because the outercoat isn't being cut away. Using a stripping knife changes the color a bit but not nearly as much as grooming with clippers does. (A show dog *must* be hand-stripped. A knife may be used, but clippers are an absolute no-no for a pet competing in conformation.)

Performing this task entirely by hand is the traditional way to strip a Miniature Schnauzer's coat, but it can take a while to learn this technique. In the meantime, you may find that a stripping knife is an easier option for you and a more comfortable choice for your dog. If you want to learn how to hand-strip properly, observe a professional breeder or groomer perform this task. Even experienced groomers may use a stripping knife, though, because it is faster than performing the task by hand.

Rest assured that when done properly, hand-stripping is not painful or uncomfortable for dogs in any way. The hair you will be removing is at the end of its growth cycle. It just needs a little push—or pull, rather—from you. You can test your dog to make sure that the coat is blown by gently tugging on the fur to see how easily it comes out. If you are unsure if you can hand-strip your Miniature Schnauzer correctly, this task may be better left to a professional groomer.

How to Hand-Strip

As you did when brushing him, place your Miniature Schnauzer on a firm, level surface, such as a grooming table.

1. Place one hand firmly on your pet so that he doesn't move when you start the hand-stripping process.
2. Next, grasp a small amount of fur between your thumb and index finger. If you are using a stripping knife, use the knife to help you gather the fur before placing your thumb on the underside of the tool.
3. Pull the fur out in one swift, straight motion. Unlike brushing, hand-stripping should always be done in the direction of the hair growth. If you are having trouble holding onto the hair, try using some grooming chalk or grooming powder. If you cut the fur with your knife, adjust the position of the tool so that it is parallel with your dog's coat.
4. The first section of hair that you strip will be in an inverted V-shape, beginning behind the dog's head and neck and widening gradually to his bottom and the backs of his hind legs. Skip the tail during the first session; that comes later.
5. The second section, which should be done about a week later, will include the sides of the neck, the remaining shoulder area, and the tail.
6. The third section should be done the following week and will consist of the remaining head area, including the cheeks and ears.

HOW TO TRIM THE EYEBROWS

A Miniature Schnauzer's eyebrows should be trimmed about once every six weeks. Although the breed's signature brows look fancy, they are surprisingly easy to achieve, providing you keep up with trims.

1. Begin by combing each eyebrow forward a couple of times.
2. Next, hold the hair from one brow on the comb as you position the tool on an angle. The shorter end should be near the inside corner of your dog's eye.
3. Then, keeping the comb between your pet and the scissors, cut the hair on this same angle. Using the comb as a cutting guide will help to protect your pet's peepers from injury, but always use the utmost care when using scissors around him, especially near his face.

BATHING

No matter how often you brush your Miniature Schnauzer or how you care for his coat, he will need regular baths to stay clean. Most Mini Schnauzers will need a bath about once every four to six weeks. If your dog gets dirty from spending a lot of time outdoors, you can bathe him as often as once a week. You needn't worry about drying out his skin as long as you use a high-quality canine shampoo and rinse it from his hair completely.

How to Bathe

Brushing should always be your first step when it comes to bathing your Miniature Schnauzer. If he has any snarls or mats, they will be significantly more difficult to remove once they are wet. Once you have brushed your pet, gather at least two large towels, a washcloth, an absorbent bath mat, his shampoo (and conditioner, if you use this product), and a couple of cotton balls.

1. Place a cotton ball in each of your dog's ears before running his bath water. The cotton will prevent water from getting into his ear canal during rinsing.
2. Instead of filling the tub with water, I recommend using your shower's hose-style attachment or a cup to wet your dog's fur. If he dislikes baths, waiting for the water to drain so that you can rinse him will only make the bath longer and his frustration more intense. Use your hand to make sure that the temperature is just right before spraying the water onto your pet.
3. First wash his face. All you will need for this part of the job is his washcloth and a bit of warm water. Avoid using shampoo on your dog's face to prevent the soap from getting into his eyes.

4. Next, dispense a small amount of shampoo into your palm and rub your hands together. Dog shampoo doesn't lather as much as human shampoo, but it will clean your dog's hair just fine. Check the package directions to see if the product can be diluted.

5. Work the shampoo into a light lather over your dog's entire body and legs. I like to use the washcloth for the dog's underside and bottom.

6. Next, turn the sprayer back on. Check the temperature once more before rinsing the shampoo from your dog's coat. To avoid rinsing shampoo onto areas you have already sprayed, begin with the back of your dog's neck and back and work downward toward his feet. The best way to be sure you have removed all the soap is by rinsing your pet twice.

7. Once you have shut off the water, run your hands over your Miniature Schnauzer gently to squeeze as much water from his coat as you can. By "wringing out" the hair on your dog's legs, you will save him a ton of drying time. Just be sure not to squeeze so hard that you hurt your pet.

8. Another way to remove excess water from your dog's coat is by holding up a towel and waiting for him to shake before removing him from the tub. Shaking after a bath is second nature for most dogs.

9. After you lift your pet from the tub, use a towel to gently squeeze the water from his coat. Resist the urge to rub him all over, as doing so can cause hair breakage and matting.

10. If you haven't already done so, you can remove the cotton from your dog's ears now.

11. Finish by brushing your pet from head to tail. A show dog usually looks best when his owner continues to brush him while blowing his coat with a hairdryer, but as long as your home is warm, your Miniature Schnauzer may enjoy air drying. Either way, brush your dog one final time once his coat is completely dry.

Hair brushing should always come before bathing your Miniature Schnauzer.

DENTAL CARE

Dog owners should brush their dogs' teeth every day. Even once or twice a week, however, is better than not brushing at all, as the condition of your Miniature Schnauzer's teeth and gums can have a considerable effect on his overall health. Even hard food leaves residue that must be brushed away to prevent plaque and tartar.

Bear in mind that your dog swallows bacteria that accumulate in his mouth, allowing these germs to enter his bloodstream. Canine periodontal disease exacerbates chronic conditions and can cause health problems when bacteria reach important organs like your dog's heart.

HOW TO CARE FOR THE TEETH

Although some dogs dislike having their teeth brushed, the biggest factor in your pet's reaction to this task is how often you expose him to it. If your dog balks at the sight of a brush, use a finger brush or even a square of damp gauze instead.

1. Dispense a pea-sized amount of toothpaste to whichever type of "brush" you use.
2. Gently lift your dog's upper lip and begin brushing his teeth in an oval motion.
3. Pay particular attention to the area where the teeth meet the gums, but don't forget the chewing surfaces. Don't bear down too hard, but do apply some pressure—at least as much as you would when brushing your own teeth.
4. Continue until you have brushed all of your Miniature Schnauzer's upper teeth. The ones in the back will be the hardest to reach, but it is important that you clean those teeth as well.
5. Next, move on to your dog's lower teeth, brushing all of them as well.

Canine toothpaste doesn't need to be rinsed off your dog's teeth and it is completely safe for him to swallow. Nonetheless, he may appreciate a cool drink of water when you finish brushing his teeth.

EAR CARE

Fortunately, neither Miniature Schnauzers with cropped ears nor those with natural ears are prone to ear infections. Nonetheless, your dog's ears should be cleaned regularly to

BE AWARE!
If your dog has an excessive amount of tartar on his teeth, you may want to schedule a professional cleaning with his veterinarian, especially if your dog has broken or loose teeth. The time to make this appointment is while your dog is still healthy. If you wait too long, he may develop a disease that makes elective procedures requiring anesthesia inadvisable.

Daily brushing is the best way to keep your dog's teeth and gums healthy.

remove dirt and excessive wax. (A clean ear shouldn't have a strong odor. It should also look pink—never red or black—on the inside.) Perform an ear cleansing every two or three weeks. You may find that your bathtub is the best spot for performing this grooming task.

HOW TO CARE FOR THE EARS

Begin by gathering your ear-cleaning supplies. You will need cleanser, cotton balls, and a hand towel. Many cleansers found in pet-supply stores contain alcohol. Alcohol speeds drying, but it can also burn your pet if he has any tiny scratches or if he simply has sensitive skin.

1. Squirt a moderate amount of cleanser into each ear. Most dogs react to the squirt by shaking their head. This actually helps loosen the debris within the ear. If your pet shakes cleanser onto you or your surroundings, use the hand towel to wipe it up.

2. Next, rub the ears gently to help distribute the cleanser. Unlike the squirt, this part should feel good to your pet. He may even lean into your hand as you rub. This is loosening the dirt and excess wax, so indulge him.

3. Using one cotton ball at a time, gently wipe the inside of each ear. You mustn't be rough, but since your Miniature Schnauzer's ear canal is L-shaped, you don't have to worry about coming into contact with the ear drum. Do not use cotton swabs, however, as these could injure him if he moves around too much.

4. Keep wiping the ear until the cotton comes out clean. It doesn't have to be pristine white, but it also shouldn't be excessively dirty. Leaving just a bit of wax behind will help to keep the ear healthy.

Praise your dog for his cooperation throughout the ear cleaning process. Once you have finished cleaning both ears, reward him with an edible treat. If he intensely dislikes having his ears cleaned, offer him a separate treat for each ear.

EYE CARE

Caring for your Miniature Schnauzer's eyes is one of the easiest of all grooming tasks. Cleaning the eyes regularly can also prevent tearstains, brownish marks under the eyes caused by discharge. If your pet suffers from tearstains, purchase tearstain remover at your local pet-supply store and apply it after each cleaning. You must remove all the matter before dealing with stains, however.

Always inspect your Miniature Schnauzer's eyes before cleaning them. Excessive redness and green or yellow discharge are signs of an infection. If you suspect an infection, skip the cleaning and make an appointment with your veterinarian. Cleaning an infected eye can hurt your pet and make it difficult for the vet to diagnose the problem.

HOW TO CARE FOR THE EYES

1. Simply wipe your pet's face a couple of times each week with a soft, damp cloth. If your pet is prone to eye discharge or tearstaining, you may need to perform this task daily instead. Allowing matter to accumulate on your dog's face is not only uncomfortable for him but can also lead to eye infections.
2. If your dog has crusty matter in the corners of his eyes, saturate your cloth with warm water. Wring the cloth out slightly to prevent dripping and then hold it over the area to soften the matter. Be careful about temperature. If the cloth feels too hot to your hand, it is too hot for your pet's face.
3. Gently wipe the area surrounding each eye. Even if your dog doesn't have visible eye discharge, wiping around his eyes regularly may prevent it from forming. You can reduce both eye discharge and tearstaining by keeping the hair surrounding your Miniature Schnauzer's eyes trimmed properly—the hair shouldn't fall into the eyes or interfere with your pet's vision.

NAIL CARE

You will need to trim your Miniature Schnauzer's toenails once every few weeks. Frequent trimming actually makes the task safer because it causes the quick—the sensitive tissue inside the nail—to recede. The exact timetable depends on how fast your dog's nails grow, his activity level, and where he exercises. Dogs who walk or run on pavement or concrete tend to wear their nails down more quickly than canine couch potatoes do.

If you can hear your Miniature Schnauzer's toenails when he walks across a floor, he is overdue for a trim. Trimmed toenails not only look better than overgrown nails, but they also feel better to your pet. Walking on nails that are too long can be painful and lead to toenails getting caught on carpet, clothing, or another pet's fur, and even pulled completely out.

Once you get the hang of nail trimming, it can be a quick and easy grooming task. In the beginning, though, the risk of cutting your pet's quick may intimidate you. If this is the case, ask his veterinarian or groomer to demonstrate a nail trim for you. You may even want to try performing the task in front of one of these professionals so that she can guide you.

HOW TO TRIM THE NAILS

Before beginning your Miniature Schnauzer's nail trim, make sure that you have styptic powder or a styptic pencil nearby. If you do cut the quick, you may need this coagulant right away. The only other things you will need are your dog and his nail clippers.

1. With your dog standing, grasp one of his paws with one of your hands. Gently press on the first paw pad to extend the nail. This step makes the nail easier to see. It also helps to keep the area still.
2. Holding your clippers in your other hand, snip off just the tiny hook-like end of the nail. If you are unsure of how much of the nail to remove, remember that you can always take a little more, but you cannot reattach what you have removed. Even if you think that you took off too little of the nail, move on to the next nail for now. Frequent shorter trims are the best way to get your pet used to clipping. They are also safer for your pet than extreme trims.
3. Continue clipping one nail at a time until you have finished all the nails on your dog's foot. When you have finished one foot, move on to the other three.
4. Check to see whether your dog still has his dewclaws. These nails are situated higher on the foot than the other nails. While they serve no practical purpose, dewclaws can get caught just as easily as your pet's other nails and should be trimmed for this reason.

Praise your dog for his compliance throughout the trimming process. Depending on how much positive reinforcement he needs, you can choose to give him an edible reward after each foot or once you have completed the entire task. Either way, be sure to give him a treat for his tolerance and consider taking him for a brisk walk, which will be fun for both of you and have a smoothing effect on any rough edges of your pet's newly trimmed nails.

HOW TO FIND A PROFESSIONAL GROOMER

As your Miniature Schnauzer's owner, you should be able to perform all the basic tasks involved in grooming him. Just because you know how to do them all, however, doesn't mean that you should have to do them yourself all the time. Professional groomers save you a great deal of time and work and show your dog that you aren't the only person who can be entrusted with his grooming needs (helpful if for any reason you cannot groom your dog yourself).

To find the best groomers in your area, all you need to do is make a few phone calls. Start by asking dog-owning friends and relatives where they take their pets. Ask how much they pay, what is typically included in this fee, and if they have ever had a bad experience (and if so, how it was handled). Mistakes happen occasionally, but the nature of the problem and how it was resolved can make a big difference. You can also call your veterinarian's office, humane society, or pet supply store. Don't be afraid to ask for references—and don't forget to check them. Membership in a grooming organization, such as the National Dog Groomers Association of America (NDGAA), is a plus.

Visit the groomer's shop in person to make your dog's first appointment. Doing so will give you a chance to see—and smell—the facility. The salon should look and smell inviting. Even more important, though, is how the staff treats the animals. Do the employees truly seem to enjoy working with the animals? If the answer to this question isn't yes, keep looking.

Trimmed toenails not only look better than overgrown nails, but they also feel better to your pet.

CHAPTER
6

HEALTH OF YOUR
MINIATURE SCHNAUZER

Virtually everything you do to care for your Miniature Schnauzer plays a role in keeping him happy and healthy, including choosing the right vet. Not only will your vet help you make important decisions about your puppy's physical health, but she will also be there to offer advice on other important aspects of pet ownership, such as training and dealing with problem behaviors.

FINDING A VETERINARIAN

You have many choices when it comes to selecting a veterinarian for your Miniature Schnauzer, but there are a few things you can do to narrow down your list of candidates. The best time to start this legwork is before you bring your new dog home so that you won't have to scramble to find someone to perform your pet's first checkup.

Begin by calling your local humane society, which can provide you with a list of local veterinarians. You can also find these names by flipping through your local yellow pages or running a quick Internet search, but even the Internet may not weed out businesses with bad reputations the way the humane society can.

Another smart way to find the most popular vets in your area is by asking family, friends, and neighbors for recommendations. Also ask why they recommend a particular person or practice. Your best bets are the veterinarians they suggest with enthusiasm. Some veterinary practices have websites that provide staff bios. This background information may also figure into your decision making.

SCHEDULE AN APPOINTMENT

If you think that you've found the right vet for your Miniature Schnauzer, the next step is stopping by to schedule an appointment. By arriving unannounced, you will get to witness a typical day at the practice. Is the waiting room crowded? Do the receptionist and veterinary technicians appear to be juggling more than they can handle? Too many people in the waiting room can mean the hospital overbooks its appointments, and understaffed practices are more likely to make mistakes that could affect your dog's health. If everything seems to be running efficiently, go ahead and make your appointment.

The facilities should be clean and well organized, but the building and furniture don't have to be expensive or fancy. One luxury many dog owners do appreciate is separate waiting rooms for pets visiting the vet for wellness exams and animals that are sick. Other factors that might affect your decision are whether your puppy will see the same veterinarian each time he visits, how the vets view holistic therapies, and whether the hospital provides 24-hour care for pets who have to stay overnight. In my opinion, overnight supervision is a must for pets required to remain at the hospital after hours.

What matters most is that you are comfortable with the veterinarian you select. Your puppy should also like his vet, but don't worry too much if that takes him some time. Veterinary checkups can be scary business for a young dog. You can help your puppy form a positive impression of the veterinary practice you

One of the most important decisions you will make for your Miniature Schnauzer puppy is which vaccinations you should ask his veterinarian to give him.

You can lessen your
Miniature Schnauzer
puppy's chances of
contracting parvovirus
by keeping him away
from public places
frequented by dogs.

choose by taking along some of his favorite treats for the staff members to offer
him. If you get a bad feeling about a specific vet or practice, however, or if your
Miniature Schnauzer puppy shows intense dislike for a particular vet, it is probably
best to continue your search.

THE ANNUAL WELLNESS EXAM

Your Miniature Schnauzer needs to visit his veterinarian at least once every
year. After weighing your dog, a veterinary technician will lead you to the
room where your dog's exam will be performed. The vet tech will then ask you
questions about your pet's health and behavior since his last checkup. As your
dog's caretaker, you know better than anyone how much he eats, how often he
sleeps, how frequently he eliminates, and how his coat looks when it's at its best.
Notifying her about changes in behavior or appearance could help identify a
health problem before it becomes a serious issue for your pet.

When the veterinarian joins you, she may begin by asking if you have any
concerns about your pet's health before checking him for signs of illness. She
will then examine his eyes, ears, nose, and mouth, listen to his heart and lungs,
examine his coat and skin, and feel the lymph nodes and internal organs. While

your vet is doing these things, she is also assessing your dog's overall demeanor. An animal's behavior is one of the best indications of how he is feeling.

If your dog appears to be happy and healthy, the vet will then confirm which vaccinations your pet is due to receive and administer them. If you still have questions that she hasn't addressed, now is the time to bring them up. The purpose of the visit is to keep your pet healthy, so any concerns relating to his health are important and relevant. If your vet tries to rush you through your dog's annual exams, it might be time to start looking for a new one.

VACCINATIONS

One of the most important decisions you will make for your Miniature Schnauzer is which vaccinations you should ask his veterinarian to give him. The exact combination of vaccines that a puppy needs depends on many factors, including where he lives, what activities he participates in, and his owner's lifestyle and frequent pastimes. Vaccines are broken into two basic types: core and noncore.

CORE VACCINES

The following vaccines are recommended for all dogs unless they have a specific medical condition that makes being vaccinated inadvisable.

Distemper: Puppies are the most susceptible to this deadly virus. Symptoms include coughing, sneezing, a thick mucus discharge from the eyes or nose, extreme weakness, and possibly seizures. There is no cure for canine distemper. Veterinarians treat its symptoms while the virus runs its course. Some dogs are able to survive distemper, but a puppy's immune system can be hard-pressed to fight this virus. A Miniature Schnauzer should receive his first distemper shot between six and nine weeks of age, and a second vaccination two to four weeks after the first. Canine distemper is passed through contact with bodily fluids, so do not allow your Miniature Schnauzer to drink from public water bowls and keep him away from strange dogs until he has been fully vaccinated.

Parvovirus: Highly contagious and often deadly without prompt treatment, parvovirus is passed through infected fecal matter. It can be contracted in public places and carried on people's hands and shoes. Symptoms include bloody diarrhea, loss of appetite, vomiting, and rapid weight loss. Although there is no cure, intravenous fluids and antibiotics can help reverse dehydration. Your Miniature Schnauzer will probably receive the parvo vaccine in a combination shot with the distemper vaccine, and should receive this vaccination annually.

Rabies: Rabies is passed through the saliva of infected animals. Any warm-blooded animal can become infected, and except for some human cases, rabies is always fatal in unvaccinated animals. Symptoms include intense aggression (sometimes with foaming at the mouth) or extreme weakness, lack of coordination, and paralysis. Rabies can take up to a month to develop, but once apparent, symptoms intensify quickly. If your puppy is bitten by another dog, ask the owner for the animal's most recent rabies vaccination paperwork right away. If a wild animal attacks your pup, take him to the vet immediately, even if the wound doesn't look serious. The only humane treatment for this disease is euthanasia.

A puppy can't receive his first rabies vaccination until he is 12 weeks old. He will need a follow-up vaccine one year from the original vaccination. After this booster shot, he will need to be revaccinated according to his municipal or state's law.

NONCORE VACCINES

"Noncore vaccines" is an umbrella term for the shots that aren't necessary for all dogs. Deciding whether to vaccinate for the following diseases is a matter of carefully weighing your pet's risk for the illness against the possible side effects of the vaccine.

Bordetella: Better known as "kennel cough," bordetella commonly affects dogs who spend time in close proximity to other dogs. Fortunately, kennel cough

A puppy can't receive his first rabies vaccination until he is 12 weeks old.

usually isn't serious. This bacterial infection causes a raspy cough and often lasts about three weeks. Most cases don't require medical treatment, but your puppy will need treatment with antibiotics if he has a fever, is at risk of developing pneumonia, or if he stops eating. If you know that your Miniature Schnauzer

puppy will be spending time around other dogs, it is wise to get him vaccinated. Some kennel cough vaccines only last about six months, so your dog may need repeated boosters if he continues to spend time around groups of other dogs.

Coronavirus: Transmitted through infected fecal matter, coronavirus affects the small intestines. Your Miniature Schnauzer can contract coronavirus by licking his paws after walking through an area where a dog with the illness has defecated. Although the disease is usually not life threatening, it can be fatal to weak, unhealthy puppies. Symptoms include vomiting and diarrhea, but healthy adult dogs may show no symptoms at all. There is no cure, but owners can make their pets more comfortable by keeping them calm and properly hydrated while they recover.

Leptospirosis: Leptospirosis is a dangerous bacterial infection spread through infected urine, bite wounds, or the ingestion of infected tissue. Acute infections can cause fever, shivering, and extreme muscle tenderness. Other symptoms include mild fever, loss of appetite, dehydration, increased thirst, and vomiting. Over time this disease can destroy the dog's kidney and liver functions. Dogs with leptospirosis are treated with strong antibiotics and fluids. Help prevent the spread of this disease, which can be passed to human family members, by not allowing your dog to drink from puddles and by keeping him away from wild animals, either alive or dead.

Puppies can be vaccinated as early as 15 weeks of age. Because the vaccine has a higher risk of side effects than many other shots, however, you should carefully consider whether this vaccine is necessary for your pet. Your vet can tell you how many cases of lepto she has been seeing in your area to help determine your dog's need for this particular vaccine.

Lyme disease: Spread by the deer tick, Lyme disease attacks multiple systems within the body. Symptoms include a mild fever and swollen joints. In more advanced cases, there may be heart and kidney inflammation. Dogs diagnosed with Lyme disease are placed on antibiotics. If you live in the northeastern, mid-Atlantic, or north-central United States and your Miniature Schnauzer spends regular time outdoors, you should talk to his veterinarian about getting him vaccinated. Even if you live elsewhere, it may be wise to vaccinate your pet if he spends a lot of time outside.

Parainfluenza: Parainfluenza spreads easily and causes fever, runny eyes and nose, and a persistent cough. It can be mild or serious. Veterinarians treat the virus with antibiotics and antiviral medications. If your dog participates in organized activities or visits a dog park regularly, you may want to consider vaccinating him against this illness. It may also be a good idea to vaccinate him if he has suffered from a severe case of parainfluenza in the past.

PARASITES

The word "parasite" refers to any type of organism that exists by feeding off other living things. Some are external parasites, and others are internal parasites. Both types can make your Miniature Schnauzer very sick.

EXTERNAL PARASITES

External parasites are parasites that attack the outside of your dog's body.

Fleas

A minor case of fleas may only cause mild skin irritation, but these tiny insects can also cause serious problems like anemia. Fleas can even

If your Miniature Schnauzer spends regular time outdoors, talk to his veterinarian about getting him vaccinated for Lyme disease.

carry tapeworms. If your dog is scratching excessively, there is a good chance that he has fleas. To find out for sure, grab a flea comb and check his coat, especially near his ears, neck, abdomen, and the base of his tail. Afterward, wipe the comb with a damp paper towel. If the tool leaves behind reddish-brown specks, you can assume that you are dealing with a flea problem.

Many medications used for treating flea infestations contain dangerous chemicals, so careful selection is essential. A bath or two with an anti-flea shampoo may be enough to rid your pet of these pests in rare cases, but you will probably need to spray your home and yard to kill fleas, eggs, and larvae in your pet's environment. Fleas can hide in carpeting, draperies, furniture—even bedding. After you have treated your dog and your home, vacuum your entire living space. Be sure to toss the vacuum bag when you are finished. You can prevent fleas by giving your pet a monthly topical flea-and-tick preventive. Fleas can still jump onto your pet, of course, but they won't survive long enough to cause a problem.

Mites

Ear mites are microscopic arachnids that can cause health problems such as abscesses, bacterial infections, and hematomas on your dog's ear flap. Symptoms of mites are excessive ear itching, head shaking, and a brownish black discharge in earwax. Left untreated, they can lead to permanent hearing loss.

After diagnosing the problem, your veterinarian will provide you with a medication. If you have other dogs (or cats) in the household, check them as well because mites are highly contagious. Since mites can live all over the body, give each pet a bath with a flea shampoo. Pay special attention to your dog's tail, as dogs are known for curling up into a ball when they sleep, with their tails close to their ears.

Ringworm

Ringworm is a fungus that attacks dogs through their hair follicles. The most obvious symptom is a small round lesion on the dog's skin. The skin at the center may look dry and scaly. Over time this lesion will get bigger with small pustules on its surface. If your dog is healthy and only has only a single lesion, your veterinarian may consider medical treatment unnecessary. A minor ringworm sore will usually resolve on its own within about a month. Otherwise, your vet will probably prescribe an antifungal cream.

Because dogs can pass this ringworm to human family members, owners should wash their hands after handling an infected pet. Young children are the most susceptible to catching ringworm, so limiting contact between your dog and your

You can prevent fleas by giving your pet a monthly topical flea-and-tick preventive.

kids is also a smart safety precaution. Ringworm fungus can survive for a year or more, so clean your dog's environment thoroughly.

Ticks

The best-known illness caused by ticks is Lyme disease, but others include babesiosis, ehrlichiosis, and Rocky Mountain spotted fever. Help your dog avoid ticks by using a topical flea preventive that also works on ticks. Also check your pet thoroughly every time he spends time in a wooded area. Remove ticks by placing tweezers around the tick, close to the head, as you gently pull it away from your dog's body. Be careful not to squeeze too tightly or twist when pulling. Once you have removed the tick, drop it in a small amount of rubbing alcohol to kill it before cleaning your pet's wound with fresh alcohol on a cotton ball and washing your hands. Ideally, use a small glass jar with a cover for the alcohol so that you can take the tick to the veterinary hospital when you have your dog examined later that day.

INTERNAL PARASITES

Internal parasites accost your pet from the inside of his body.

Heartworms

Heartworms cause hypertension, secondary health issues, and ultimately heart failure. They are spread through bites from mosquitoes that carry the illness. It is important to give your dog a monthly heartworm preventive (which also protects against other internal parasites, such as hookworms and roundworms) regardless of where you live. When used correctly, the medication is nearly 100 percent effective, but a single missed dose can result in a deadly infection.

Even with year-round prevention, have your Miniature Schnauzer tested for heartworm disease at least once a year. Most dogs show no symptoms until the disease has progressed to a serious stage. Symptoms then include coughing, difficulty breathing, and marked exercise intolerance. The prognosis for an infected dog depends on several factors, including age, overall health, and medical response time. Heartworm treatment is much safer than it used to be, but prevention is highly preferable.

Hookworms

The hookworm is named for the tiny hooks around the mouth that allow it to attach to the wall of the dog's intestine and suck blood. Hookworms are often passed to puppies from their mother's placenta or milk and to adult dogs through

Heartworm preventives are nearly 100 percent effective and help to prevent the disease throughout the year when taken monthly.

contact with infected fecal matter. Symptoms include bloody diarrhea, itching, weight loss and sometimes extreme fatigue due to anemia.

Hookworms can be deadly in severe cases, but they present the biggest threat to puppies and adult dogs with other health issues. Your vet will treat hookworms with a deworming medication. Several doses may be necessary. Although over-the-counter medications are available, it is smarter to seek veterinary treatment.

Roundworms
Roundworms grow up to four to five inches (10–12 cm) in length and attack a dog's intestinal tract. Signs of roundworms include colic, lethargy, loss of appetite, vomiting, abdominal swelling, worms in stool, and sometimes persistent coughing. A dog with a severe infestation may also experience anorexia. A deworming medication may be sufficient for treating a minor case of roundworms, but again, visit your vet instead of using an over-the-counter medicine. Several follow-up visits to the vet may be necessary. In more severe situations, surgery may be necessary.

Tapeworms
Tapeworms are named for their flat, tape-like appearance. They can be anywhere from a single inch (2.5 cm) to several feet (m) in length and attach themselves to the wall of your dog's small intestine. Dogs can become infested with tapeworms when they ingest fleas carrying the parasites or eat raw meat that has been infested. If your dog does become the host of a tapeworm, you may see body segments in his feces or crawling around the fur near your dog's anus. Many dogs also experience itching in this area. Fortunately, your vet can usually eradicate this parasite with one dose of deworming medication.

Whipworms
Whipworms are named for their whip-like appearance. They are typically between 2 and 3 inches (50 and 76 cm) long and attach themselves to the lining of the intestinal wall. Whipworm eggs are then shed through an infected animal's feces. The most common symptom of a severe infestation is bloody diarrhea, but dogs with fewer worms may show no signs of illness. Several deworming medications are available, but multiple treatments may be necessary. Because diagnosis can be tricky, bring a stool sample from your pet whenever you visit the vet.

GENERAL ILLNESSES

The following health problems commonly affect all breeds.

ALLERGIES

If your dog is itching and scratching constantly and you have ruled out external parasites, an allergy may be the problem. Most canine allergies are inhalant allergies (pollen, dust, mold, etc.). Food allergies are also common, with prevalent allergens including beef, corn, dairy products, soybeans, and wheat. Your veterinarian can perform allergy testing to pinpoint the problem food, but this can be expensive and inaccurate. Instead, she may suggest placing your dog on a hypoallergenic diet to help alleviate the itching. The next step is usually an elimination diet, which means cooking for your pet and eliminating different ingredients every few weeks in hopes of isolating the offending food.

CANCER

Cancer is the most common cause of disease-related deaths in dogs. At one time a diagnosis of cancer was an automatic death sentence, but more and more dogs are surviving this disease. In addition to improving technology, another reason

for these success stories is early diagnosis. Symptoms of cancer are just as numerous as the varieties of the disease, but some of the most common include loss of appetite, persistent lameness, tumors, and weight loss. These are really just the tip of the iceberg, though. If you think your dog seems less like himself, even if you can't put your finger on what exactly is different, it may be worth discussing with your vet.

If your dog is diagnosed with cancer, your vet may be able to help him through a variety

Consistent itching and scratching may mean that your dog has inhalant or food allergies.

of treatments. The prognosis depends on many different factors, including your dog's age, the type of cancer, and when you discovered it. Surgery and chemotherapy are often the most effective choice, but nutritional support, pain management, physical therapy, and even acupuncture have been shown to make a very real difference in many situations.

EAR INFECTIONS

Miniature Schnauzers are less prone to ear infections than breeds with longer ears, but they can still get them if you don't make regular ear cleanings a priority. Your dog may be suffering from an ear infection if he is tilting or shaking his head or scratching his ears in response to obvious discomfort. If you witness these behaviors, take a look inside his ear. The interior should be pink. If it is red or swollen or there is black or yellowish discharge, your dog may have an ear infection. Infected ears often have a strong, offensive odor.

If you suspect that your dog has an ear infection, make an appointment with his veterinarian. Do not clean the ear, as this may be painful for your pet and can make it more difficult for the vet to diagnose the problem. Your vet will need to examine your pet to rule out a ruptured eardrum before prescribing an antibiotic. Because some ear infections can lead to hearing loss, it is important to continue giving your dog his medication for the duration of time recommended by your vet.

EYE INFECTIONS

Eye infections aren't common in Miniature Schnauzers, but some dogs do suffer an occasional case of conjunctivitis, or pink eye. Symptoms include redness, discharge, and pawing at the eye in response to discomfort. Pink eye isn't serious. Your vet will most likely prescribe eye drops or ointment. As long as you follow the directions, the problem should be resolved within a week or two.

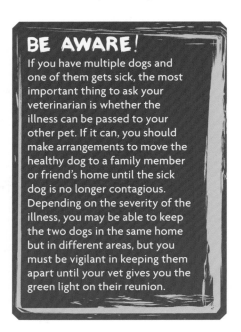

BE AWARE!
If you have multiple dogs and one of them gets sick, the most important thing to ask your veterinarian is whether the illness can be passed to your other pet. If it can, you should make arrangements to move the healthy dog to a family member or friend's home until the sick dog is no longer contagious. Depending on the severity of the illness, you may be able to keep the two dogs in the same home but in different areas, but you must be vigilant in keeping them apart until your vet gives you the green light on their reunion.

ALTERNATIVE THERAPIES

Alternative medicine goes by many different names and includes modalities that are frequently referred to as types of holistic medicine, meaning that they treat the whole being instead of just one particular illness. Many veterinarians who practice alternative modalities prefer the term "complementary medicine" because these methods can be used in conjunction with traditional approaches.

I recommend learning about these lesser-known options and utilizing the ones that make sense to you. If a particular type of treatment seems like a bad idea to you or your veterinarian, though, there is no reason you must try it. Complementary medicine isn't something to try because everyone else is doing it.

ACUPUNCTURE

This ancient Chinese modality is based on the premise that each part of the body corresponds to a different acupuncture point. Acupuncturists stimulate specific points with tiny needles to trigger healing in the related areas. Acupuncture needles are almost as thin as a human hair, and the majority of people who have undergone acupuncture treatments assert that the procedure is remarkably painless.

Acupuncture is commonly used for treating a multitude of canine illnesses, including gastrointestinal disorders, kidney disease, musculoskeletal disorders, neurological disorders, respiratory conditions, skin diseases, thyroid disorders, and even urinary incontinence. Although there is no guarantee that acupuncture will help your Miniature Schnauzer with his specific health issue, one of the biggest advantages of trying this modality is that it poses no side effects.

HERBAL MEDICINE

When wild animals are sick, they seem to know exactly which plants to eat to cure what ails them. Herbal medicine is based on the premise that there is a natural remedy for every kind of illness. If you want to try an herbal approach, talk to your veterinarian. If she doesn't practice herbal medicine herself, she may be able to suggest a reliable herbalist. Unless this person is also a veterinarian, be sure that your vet remains involved in your dog's treatment plan.

Never give your dog any herb or supplement, no matter how harmless it may seem, without your vet's prior approval. Certain herbs that are safe for humans are not safe for dogs. Even herbs that are safe for dogs can cause problems when given in conjunction with other medications or if certain health problems are present.

HOMEOPATHY

The premise of homeopathy is that like cures like. If your dog is suffering from an illness, a homeopathic veterinarian may suggest introducing the agent that caused the illness to alleviate it (an approach similar to the concept of vaccination). The best homeopathic practitioners are also veterinarians, but again, if you work with someone who isn't a vet, involve your veterinarian in your dog's treatment.

Homeopathy is not something in which anyone should dabble. If you think that a homeopathic remedy might help your dog with

Dog Tale

I was once a skeptic myself, but then I witnessed the healing effects of acupuncture when one of my dogs ruptured his anterior cruciate ligament. Because he was overweight, my dog wasn't a good candidate for surgery, but in the same time it would have taken him to recover from the operation, acupuncture helped heal his injury. I ended up saving my dog a great deal of pain by remaining open to this less conventional form of treatment.

a specific problem, talk to your vet. The right veterinarian for your pet will listen to your concerns and suggestions and help you make sound decisions to keep him healthy.

PHYSICAL THERAPY/ TTOUCH®

Physical therapy is typically considered one of the more mainstream types of complementary veterinary medicine. It's most often used to help animals heal from neurological problems, orthopedic injuries, or surgical procedures. If your dog needs physical therapy, look for a caregiver who is both a veterinarian and a licensed physical therapist for people. Currently, there is no licensing program for canine physical therapists, so it's especially important that the therapist you choose has a solid understanding of the ways the canine body differs from the human body.

Never perform any type of physical therapy on your pet without the advice of a professional caregiver. Even massage can worsen an injured pet's condition if it isn't performed correctly. A specific variety of physical therapy involving massage is called Tellington TTouch, or simply TTouch. Developed by a horse trainer, this technique is now used around the world for dogs as well. TTouch is known to reduce tension and is considered to be effective for improving both canine health and behavior.

CANINE FIRST-AID KIT

The following items should always be kept on hand in the event of a medical emergency:
- antibiotic ointment
- canine first-aid manual
- children's diphenhydramine (antihistamine)
- corn syrup
- cotton swabs

- emergency phone numbers (including poison control, emergency veterinarian, and your dog's regular vet)
- hydrogen peroxide
- instant ice pack
- liquid bandages
- nonstick gauze pads, gauze, and tape
- oral syringe or eyedropper
- rectal thermometer
- saline solution
- scissors
- soap
- styptic powder or pencil
- tweezers
- any other item your veterinarian recommends keeping on hand

Remember to keep an eye on expiration dates, and toss any out-of-date products.

SENIOR DOGS

Like people, dogs don't just wake up one morning and become seniors. It is a gradual process that begins in late adulthood. A Miniature Schnauzer's senior

Dog Tale

People have lied to their children about the loss of pets for so long that the old story about the family dog going to live out his days on a farm is now officially a cliché. As a mother myself, I know how painful it can be to watch your child deal with grief for the first time. I urge you, however, to face this challenge with honesty so that your child can learn how to deal with loss and sadness.

My son Alec first dealt with the loss of a pet when he was about four years old. He was sad at first, but in typical preschooler fashion, he expressed his feelings and then began to move on. He did ask if he could keep one of the pet's toys to remember him by, though. It took me a lot longer to deal with my own grief, but whenever I was feeling sad over this loss, I knew that my husband and I had done the right thing by telling Alec the truth. He would climb into my lap if I started to cry and ask, "Are you missing Johnny?" When I would nod, Alec would tell me that he missed him, too. Now years later, Alec still has that stuffed animal that belonged to Jonathan.

years begin around the time he is ten years old. The first signs of aging you may notice in your pet include decreased energy, a greater need for sleep or altered sleep patterns, and a waning appetite. In other breeds a graying muzzle accompanies these changes, but this sign may be easily missed in the Miniature Schnauzer due to his natural coloring.

Dogs who lead healthier lives tend to live longer and experience fewer health problems in general. Advancing age, however, places your Miniature Schnauzer at an increased risk for several illnesses, such as arthritis, canine cognitive dysfunction (CCD), and Cushing's disease. Older dogs are also considerably more sensitive to illnesses caused by parasites such as fleas, ticks, mosquitoes, and worms.

The best way to identify a problem before it snowballs into a bigger issue is to take your older dog for checkups more often than before. Instead of taking him for a yearly exam, schedule two wellness visits each year for your senior pet, and make sure that he receives routine blood work. Don't forget to bring a stool sample each time you take him for an appointment, routine or otherwise.

As dogs age, their metabolisms begin to slow down, causing them to gain extra weight. Carrying extra weight places your pet at an increased risk for developing arthritis, so it helps to put him on a sensible diet. Your older dog may also become more susceptible to cold and drafts. If you live in a colder climate, consider buying your dog a coat for trips outdoors when the temperatures plummet. Additionally, an older dog may experience some hearing loss. This problem tends to worsen over time, eventually resulting in complete deafness for some animals. If your older dog is starting to lose his hearing, you can begin teaching him hand signals for the commands he already knows.

A small amount of petulance is normal for an aging animal, but sudden or extreme changes in temperament can be a sign of a physical problem. If your Miniature Schnauzer seems especially irritable for no apparent reason, make an appointment with his veterinarian to rule out a medical cause. Older dogs are prone to a number of health problems, but early diagnosis can make a big difference in the prognoses of many of these illnesses.

CHAPTER 1

TRAINING YOUR MINIATURE SCHNAUZER

Both people and animals are often happiest when they are allowed to nurture their own unique set of talents. By exposing your Miniature Schnauzer to training, you just might discover some hidden talents you otherwise wouldn't have known your dog possessed. He doesn't have to compete for fancy ribbons or prestigious titles to enjoy obedience (though you just might decide that formal competition can be fun for you both), because training itself can be a lot of fun for both dogs and their owners.

WHY TRAIN YOUR MINIATURE SCHNAUZER?

Formal dog training might seem unnecessary, especially if you bought your Miniature Schnauzer to be a family companion and nothing more, but training him to perform basic commands is still a smart idea. It may surprise you that teaching your puppy a single command could save his life, but teaching him to come when called can do just that if he ever gets away from you outdoors. A well-behaved dog is also welcome in more places than one who barks and causes a ruckus, and the best way to ensure that your Miniature Schnauzer will grow into a well-mannered adult is by making training a priority when he is still young.

The Miniature Schnauzer is a very intelligent breed. Your pup will enjoy learning new things and receiving your heartfelt praise (and edible rewards)

Making training a priority can help your Miniature Schnauzer grow into a well-mannered adult.

when he makes the connection between your commands and his behavior. These dogs love to please their owners. You'll be amazed by the pride you feel when you successfully teach your dog a new command or trick.

POSITIVE TRAINING

Whether you plan to train your Miniature Schnauzer to follow simple commands or want to participate

PUPPY POINTER

Using high-value treats for rewarding your Miniature Schnauzer can make all the difference in smaintaining his interest in training. Foods like chicken or hot dogs are usually big hits with young dogs. Just be sure to cut the food into tiny pieces so that you can give him numerous rewards without an exorbitant number of calories. Since intermittent rewards work best, mix a little dry dog food into your treat bag as well. The first time your puppy sits on command, offer him a piece of kibble along with a heartfelt "Good boy!" Next, use praise alone. When he complies the third time, offer him the high-value treat.

in an organized activity together, a positive training approach is essential. Both your dog's success and the quality of your relationship with your pet depend on it. Never follow training advice, from a professional trainer or anyone else, if it seems abusive in any way.

Puppies respond best to positive reinforcement. If you reward your pup with praise and a treat, he is going to be much more likely to repeat this behavior. If you yell at him when he doesn't comply, the only thing you will teach him is to fear you. Never, under any circumstance, strike your Miniature Schnauzer. Physical punishment has no place in dog training.

Dogs are incredibly perceptive individuals. Even their owners' moods can affect their training success. If you have had a bad day or aren't feeling your best, postpone training until you are confident that you can approach the task with a positive attitude. If you are feeling frustrated or impatient—even if it has nothing to do with your puppy—he will likely pick up on these feelings. Part of your job as your dog's trainer is to set him up for success. Sometimes this means knowing when a break is necessary.

Owners who make training fun for their pets often have the most success. Puppies, like young children, can have short attention spans. Utilizing games as a means of practicing commands with your pet is a great way to make sure that

Socialization is one of the most important parts of dog training.

he's always up for a training session. For instance, play hide-and-seek as a way to practice the *come* command. Just make sure that your Miniature Schnauzer puppy always assumes the role of the seeker. (You should never teach your puppy to hide from you.)

Another important part of a positive approach is keeping training sessions short. Your pup will learn considerably more through multiple short training sessions in a given day than he will in one long session. Training sessions for young puppies should last no longer than five minutes at a time. As your pup gets older, you can lengthen the duration of his training sessions a bit, but even an older puppy shouldn't be expected to work on training any longer than 15 or 20 minutes without a break.

SOCIALIZATION

Socialization simply means introducing your puppy to as many people and other pets as possible to ensure that he continues to have positive interactions with everyone he meets. Even a friendly dog can develop problems when he isn't exposed to strangers or taught proper social etiquette. A dog who is socialized from an early age, however, will grow into a well-adjusted adult who can be taken virtually anywhere.

Socialization isn't difficult, and you may not even see its benefits right away, but overlooking this vital part of training is among the biggest mistakes new dog owners make. When you're busy, it may seem easier to leave your pup at home instead of taking him out to meet the masses, but I assure you that leaving him behind will only make his training more difficult down the road.

HOW TO SOCIALIZE

It may sound complicated, but socialization is actually one of the easiest parts of puppy training. All you have to do is make a point of taking your Miniature Schnauzer puppy with you to as many places as you can. Of course, you should wait until your puppy has had all his shots before taking him to places where numerous dogs gather, such as dog parks and pet-supply stores.

1.) Take Your Puppy Lots of Places

Take your pup with you to pick your kids up from school. Attach his leash before running over to a neighbor's to drop off a piece of mail you received by mistake. If you get an invitation to a cookout, ask the host if you may bring your puppy with you to meet everyone, or throw your own cookout and invite friends and family. Whether at home or in public, keep treats handy so that new people can offer them to your pet. It is very important that he forms a positive connotation with these interactions.

2.) Expose Your Puppy to People and Situations

Even when all your dog is doing is walking down the sidewalk amongst the crowd with nobody paying him attention, he is learning to tolerate the presence of other people. A dog who understands that people belong on sidewalks will be less inclined to bark at strangers who walk past his own home.

When you encounter people who aren't comfortable around dogs, don't force your puppy on them. In addition to respecting these people's feelings, it is important to understand that your dog is unlikely to get anything positive from a forced interaction.

CRATE TRAINING

Crate training allows you to utilize your dog's natural instinct to seek out a den as a way of keeping him safe when no one can watch him. Another advantage of crate training is its value as a housetraining aid. Most dogs possess a strong aversion to soiling the area in which they sleep. This deeply ingrained instinct helps prevent housetraining accidents for puppies who sleep in their crates.

Generally speaking, most puppies can be successfully crate trained, but a crate is a bad idea in a couple of situations. Animals raised in puppy mills spend nearly all their time in these tiny enclosures amongst their own filth. Understandably, many of these pups have an outright phobia of spending time inside a crate and shouldn't have to relive their pasts by being crated again. Another legitimate reason not to crate your Miniature Schnauzer is if you don't want to. Nothing more—

Exposing your puppy to many different people and other pets will help him feel comfortable and behave well in social situations.

that's reason enough. Countless puppies have grown into happy, healthy, and fully housetrained adult dogs without this common training device. Moreover, if you feel strongly that crating isn't right for you, your puppy will likely pick up on this stance, and it could affect the way he himself sees his crate.

HOW TO CRATE TRAIN

If you plan to train your Miniature Schnauzer to use a crate, you should begin as soon as you bring your puppy home. The first thing you need to do is introduce your pup to his new crate (or "kennel"). This step should be done in the most subtle way possible.

1.) Find the Right Spot

After assembling the crate and furnishing it with a padded liner, situate it where you plan to keep it. A quiet corner of the room, not unlike the space your pup would seek out himself, is usually an ideal spot. The crate shouldn't be placed in a location that is too remote, though. The location should be peaceful, but you don't want your pet to feel estranged from the rest of the household when he is in his kennel.

2.) Leave the Door Open

After placing a toy and an edible treat inside the crate, leave the door open. Your goal at this point is simply to make the crate inviting so that your pet will go inside to check it out. When he does venture into the kennel, hold off on praising him or you may distract him from investigating his new digs. Give him a chance to check things out, but don't forget to praise him before he comes out. If he's tired, he may decide to lie down for a while. This is the best thing that can happen.

Repeat this exercise several times over the next few days. During this warm-up period, never shut the crate door, whether your pet is inside the kennel or not. At this point your only goal is to get him to go inside the crate—he should be able to enter and exit any time he wishes. Whenever you notice that the treat has been eaten, replace it with a new one. This will help him see entering his crate as a rewarding experience.

3.) Close the Door

Once your puppy is going inside his crate on a regular basis, you can move on to closing the door for brief periods. Plan these periods for when you can remain in the same room. Your presence will be reassuring to him if closing the door causes any anxiety. Even with you right there, he may still fuss when you first close the door. This is normal, but you shouldn't respond by opening the door. If you do, what you teach your pet is that fussing gets him his own way.

The Miniature Schnauzer is an intelligent, trainable breed.

Keep the treats handy, giving them to your puppy sporadically through the closed door when he is quiet. Avoid sitting in front of the crate or focusing too much attention on your pet, which could make him start imploring to be released instead of relaxing. Only leave the door closed for two or three minutes at a time. You want to be able to praise your pet for good behavior when you open the crate door. Even if he fusses incessantly, you should wait for a break in the vocalizations before springing your pet.

4.) Lengthen the Time Inside

Once your puppy tolerates spending a few minutes inside his crate with the door closed, gradually lengthen the amount of time he spends inside. If your dog likes toys that you can stuff with treats, crate-training sessions are excellent times to offer them. You still need to remain in the room with your puppy during this phase. If you leave abruptly, it may cause him to feel insecure and regress in his training.

When your Miniature Schnauzer is spending 20 minutes or more in his crate without complaint, begin leaving the room for short periods while he's inside. Avoid hiding around the corner to see if your pet is going to start wailing as soon as you leave. Dogs have excellent hearing, so your pup may think that you are initiating a game and start fussing. Go to the kitchen for a glass of water, or get towels from the clothes dryer in the laundry room. You needn't be gone long in the beginning; in fact, it's better if you're not.

Once your puppy is comfortable with your leaving the room, gradually increase the amount of time before your return. Eventually, you will move on to leaving the house for short periods and likewise extending the duration of this absence.

BE AWARE!

Crates aren't for punishment. If you can't watch your Miniature Schnauzer when he's a puppy, place him in his crate with a favorite toy to prevent him from chewing your possessions. But don't try to teach him a lesson by putting him in his kennel after the crime. Then he will start seeing his kennel as a jail instead of a refuge. This negative connotation can reverse all the progress you have made with crate training.

MAXIMUM CRATE TIME

An eight-week-old puppy should spend no more than two hours at a time in his crate. Be sure to take him to his potty spot before placing him in his crate, and give him another opportunity to relieve himself when you let him out. If you will be leaving the house for more than a couple of hours, ask a family member to take him out for a bathroom break and some exercise. The purpose of the crate is to keep your pet safe and prevent him from having housetraining accidents when you can't watch him. The crate is not a place to keep your puppy long-term.

Adult dogs can stay in their crates longer, but they too must be let out for elimination breaks and exercise at regular intervals. If you will be gone overnight, have that same family member check in every few hours. Senior dogs may need a break after just four hours. If you work full-time, consider enrolling your pet in doggy day care, as no animal should be confined to a crate for more than six hours at a time.

HOUSETRAINING

Housetraining is about empowering your Miniature Schnauzer by teaching him the proper place for elimination. The key to successful housetraining is sticking to a schedule. Some puppies take longer to catch on than others, and most have accidents, but your Miniature Schnauzer will learn. By making your housetraining schedule a top priority, you can decrease the time it takes for your pup to become reliably housetrained.

A housetraining strategy should never be based on fear tactics. All owners accomplish by rubbing noses in accidents is ruining their relationships with their pets. A puppy who is being humiliated or hurt cannot learn anything. Your puppy doesn't want to soil his new home, but he won't know where you want him to relieve himself until you show him. Once he understands your expectations—and how happy you are when he complies with them—he will be more likely to use his potty spot for elimination instead of your living room carpet.

HOW TO HOUSETRAIN

Housetraining should begin the moment you bring your puppy home. As soon as you get out of your vehicle, take your dog to his designated potty spot. He may or may not go, although a long ride usually leads to a full bladder. Be patient with your pet. He may not even realize that he has to go until he has had a chance to sniff his surroundings and get his bearings. You can help him by reducing the amount of distraction. Ask family members to wait inside for you and your pet. If your pup eliminates, praise him and head indoors. If he doesn't go after several minutes, walk him around a bit. Many dogs will empty their bladder on a quick walk, if for no other reason than to mark territory.

If your dog still doesn't eliminate after a quick walk, go indoors so that he can start settling into his new home. Show him to his water bowl at once, and keep an eye on the clock. After about 20 minutes or so, provide him with another opportunity to eliminate. It's normal for a dog to sniff around a lot when he enters a new home, so this alone isn't necessarily a sign that your dog has to go, but moving around in circles or back-and-forth motions may mean that your pup is ready for another trip outside.

Take your puppy to his potty spot every couple of hours during his first few weeks at home. You should also take him outside as soon as he wakes up from a nap and immediately after an exercise or play session. In the beginning it may seem like all you are doing is taking your puppy outdoors, but this hard work will pay off when you can proudly say that your Miniature Schnauzer is housetrained. If you are lax about the schedule, your puppy will take longer to become fully trained.

Your puppy will probably need at least one middle-of-the-night potty break during those first few weeks. Keep in mind that as he gets a little older, his bladder will get slightly bigger. Most pups can generally go about one hour between elimination trips for each month of age. This means that when your dog is three months old, you'll only be taking him out every three hours. Once he's four months old, you'll only be trekking outside with him every four hours. This timeframe reaches a reasonable limit once your pup is between six and eight months old. Even an adult dog should be taken outside to eliminate every six to eight hours.

If you have adopted an adult dog, begin his housetraining using this same two-hour system. Depending on your pet's age and how quickly he catches on, though, he may be able to transition to longer stretches between potty breaks more quickly than a younger dog would. If you notice that your dog is only eliminating every other time you take him to his potty spot, for example, he may only need a potty break every four hours.

Praise and Timing
Praise your puppy exuberantly whenever he eliminates in the proper spot. Proper timing is essential, though. Begin your "good boys" as soon as he starts to go—no sooner—so that he is sure to understand what he is doing right. You may even offer him an edible treat when he has finished.

Scheduling
I recommend using a chart to keep track of your puppy's housetraining progress. Mark the times that your puppy eats, when he has a successful trip to his potty spot, and when he has an accident. By keeping track of this information, you will be able to pinpoint the specific times of day when your Miniature Schnauzer pup is having the most accidents.

Sometimes a simple adjustment can help your puppy succeed. Removing his water bowl a couple of hours before bedtime, for example, may help your pup make it to his potty spot in the morning. If you tend to hit the snooze button several times before getting out of bed in the morning, changing this habit could help your pup as well.

Dealing With Accidents

If your puppy has an accident, don't feel discouraged. Use this mishap as a learning opportunity for your pet. If possible, interrupt him while he is still relieving himself and take him outside immediately. If he has finished before you realized he began, remove him from the room while you clean up the mess. Your Miniature Schnauzer pup should never watch you perform cleanup duty. Witnessing this step can make some puppies assume that their job is to make the mess and their owners' job is to clean it up.

You can help show your dog where you want him to eliminate by moving a small amount of the waste from his accident to his potty spot. Use a plastic bag or pooper scooper to transport solid waste. A urine-soaked paper towel can be left at the potty spot to help show your new pet where he should urinate. As soon as your dog starts to use his potty spot, you can skip this step, but scent clues can be extremely effective. Dogs are much more likely to eliminate in an area where they have eliminated before.

If you have adopted an adult dog, housetrain him the same way you would a puppy.

Because of your Miniature Schnauzer's highly developed sense of smell, it is vital that you clean up his accidents thoroughly. If you don't, the chances of your pup having another accident in the same location rise considerably. Don't use any cleaning product that contains ammonia, as it will only encourage your pup to eliminate indoors again. Ammonia is one of the most pungent ingredients in urine.

Ensuring Continued Success

You can assume that your puppy is officially housetrained when he has gone three months without a housetraining accident. By this time you will probably be on a less rigorous schedule in regard to the number of trips you make to his potty spot each day. To ensure your pup's continued success, though, make sure that you make a point of maintaining his routine. If he begins having accidents in the house again, you must begin remedial training, which means increasing the number of trips outside.

INDOOR HOUSETRAINING

Most Miniature Schnauzer owners train their dogs to eliminate outdoors. Because these dogs are so small, however, they can be taught to use a litter box indoors. Some companies even make litter designed especially for dogs instead of cats. Housetraining a dog to eliminate indoors isn't much different from training him to go outside. While the where is obviously different, the what and the how are basically the same. You will still need to take your puppy to his potty spot when it is time for him to go, and you should still praise your pet whenever he complies.

BASIC COMMANDS

A Miniature Schnauzer is old enough to start learning a few basic commands by the time he is about five weeks of age. Begin training your pet as soon as you bring him home, working on one command at a time until he has mastered the task at hand. Use both rewards and praise until he is complying about 85 percent of the time. At this point you can then start using the treats intermittently, but always praise your pup when he follows your commands. Too many treats can cause your Miniature Schnauzer puppy to become overweight, but there is no such thing as too much praise when it is deserved.

Begin training your Miniature Schnauzer as soon as you bring him home.

COME

If you only teach your dog a single command, *come* should be it. Responding to this one word could save your Miniature Schnauzer from running away and becoming lost, getting into an altercation with an aggressive animal, or being hit by an automobile. I also find the *come* command useful at mealtime, bath time (but only if your dog likes baths), and bedtime.

How to Teach *Come*

The easiest way to teach your dog to come to you is by catching him in the act.

Dog Tale

Never use the *come* command if you are upset with your dog. If you do, you will risk lowering the chances of his responding to it in an emergency. For this same reason, I don't use the command for my dog Damon when it's time for his bath. Molly loves a bath, but Damon thinks this grooming task is a primitive form of water torture. If your puppy feels similarly, I'd skip this command at his bath times.

1. When you notice your puppy moving toward you, bend your knees and lower your body in a welcoming gesture as you say the word "come" in an upbeat tone.
2. Ideally, you should have an edible reward to offer your pet when he reaches you, but if you don't, be sure to tell him what a good boy he is.
3. You can even move to where you keep his treat container and repeat the exercise if he follows you. Most puppies learn commands more quickly when their compliance is followed by a tasty snack.

When you practice the *come* command, you must have a means of enticing your dog to come to you. Taking along some of those treats is usually enough to do the trick. It is important that your puppy equates the word with the action, though. No matter how many times you repeat the word, your puppy won't realize that it means moving toward you unless that is what he is doing when he hears it.

SIT

Teaching a puppy to sit is one of the easiest of all training tasks. Sitting is also the basis for many other commands, so it makes sense to teach it sooner rather than later. If your breeder has already taught your puppy this simple command, keep practicing it with your dog to keep it fresh in his mind.

How to Teach *Sit*

To teach the *sit* command:
1. Hold a treat in your hand as you stand in front of your pup.
2. Slowly raise the treat over his head to encourage him to move his body into

the sitting position naturally.

3. As soon as he does this, say, "Sit" so that he connects the command with its meaning.

Most puppies will sit as soon as the treat is placed over their heads. Do not push on the dog's backside, as this could injure him.

Once your pup learns how to sit on command, you can practice in numerous situations—during training sessions, at mealtimes, and before heading out the door. Many owners consider it polite for a dog to sit before having his bowl placed in front of him. Asking your puppy to sit before you take him outside not only teaches him good manners, but it also makes it easier to attach his leash.

DOWN

Use *down* to prevent your puppy from jumping on guests and for calming him when he gets too excited in general. Instead of saying "lie down," most owners simply say "down" instead. A single word is easier for your pup to understand than a longer command.

How to Teach *Down*

Teaching the *down* command is a lot like teaching *sit*.

1. With your puppy sitting, hold a treat in front of him.
2. Instead of raising it over his head, slowly lower it in front of him.
3. If he doesn't respond by lying down, move closer and lower the treat again, but don't let him have it until he lowers his whole body.
4. Say the word "down" as he does this so that he knows why you are rewarding him.

The *down* command can be used to calm your puppy when he gets overexcited.

STAY

A Miniature Schnauzer who stays on command is safer in almost any situation. *Stay* is also an important part of formal obedience trials and rally obedience. Teach your pet how to stay in both the sitting position and when lying down. A well-trained dog can stay for an extended period of time even if his owner moves out of sight, but this level of compliance takes extensive practice.

How to Teach *Stay*

1. Begin working on the *stay* command with your dog sitting.
2. Once you have commanded him to sit, back up slowly.
3. Say the word "stay" repeatedly as long as he remains sitting. Speak calmly and clearly. If your dog senses too much excitement, it could cause him to come to you. Also, refrain from giving him his treat until you walk back to him. It is essential that he is still sitting still when you give him the treat so that he understands what he has done correctly.

   In the very beginning, your Miniature Schnauzer may only stay still for a few seconds, and that is okay. What matters is that you say the command and reward him at the appropriate times. As he catches on, you will be able to back up farther—and even walk in a circle around your pet. A reasonable goal for a dog just learning the command is staying for minute or two at a time. You can lengthen the amount of time gradually as your pet masters this command.

HEEL (WALK NICELY ON LEASH)

Whether you make proper leash etiquette a priority or not, you will be reinforcing the way your pup walks on his lead every time you take him outdoors. If you tolerate habits like chewing on the lead and pulling when your dog is young, he will continue these behaviors into adulthood. It is much easier to train your puppy how to walk on a leash now than to correct leash behavior later.

The *heel* command is all about perfecting your pet's leash manners and having him walk along by your left side. A heeling dog walks when his owner walks, sits patiently when his owner stops, and resumes walking when his owner starts moving once again.

How to Teach *Heel*

Some puppies are a little scared of the leash in the very beginning, so the best way to start leash training is by letting your dog check out the lead. Place it in front of him and let him sniff it. If this goes okay, attach it and let him walk around inside the house while wearing it. Keep an eye on him so that he doesn't trip or fall down, but otherwise let him be. If he takes the leash into his mouth, take it out immediately. If he persists, offer him a toy as a replacement item.

Once your puppy seems comfortable wearing his leash, head outdoors with him. Take along some treats so that you can reward him for his good behavior and a favorite toy that is small enough for your pet to carry if you need to dissuade him from chewing on the lead again. During your puppy's first few walks, you needn't be worried about teaching him how to heel. You can tackle that once he has other basic commands under his belt. For now just practice walking with your pet—in straight lines, around corners, and up and down hills. Praise him for his cooperation, stopping to treat him occasionally.

Don't forget to change your direction once in a while to make sure that your puppy learns that he has to go where you choose. If your puppy pulls, stop immediately. It is important that he learns right away that pulling does not get him where he wants to go. If he continues to pull when you resume walking, change your direction again—and again and again—until he stops pulling.

Once your dog is comfortable walking on the leash, you can teach him the *heel* command:

1. Start by attaching your Miniature Schnauzer's leash and walking him on your left side. Make a point of stopping every so often and issuing the *sit* command.
2. Wait a few seconds before walking again, encouraging your pet to walk with you as you do.
3. Repeat these steps several times, rewarding your dog with praise and a treat each time he stops and sits. Eventually, he will sit whenever you stop, just as he sits whenever he sees you holding his food bowl.
4. Once your dog is sitting consistently whenever you stop, start saying "heel" instead of "sit." Technically, heeling means walking when you walk and sitting when you stop. Reinforcing this command will teach your dog to walk with you at your pace. You needn't say "heel" each time you stop in the future, but if he forgets his leash manners, all you will have to do is say "heel" to remind him what you expect of him.

FINDING A PROFESSIONAL TRAINER

Whether you realize it or not, you already have some wonderful resources for finding a great trainer at your disposal. Your Miniature Schnauzer's breeder and his veterinarian are two of the best people to ask for a recommendation. Chances are good that your breeder can point you toward a trainer who has worked with some of her previous Miniature Schnauzer pups. Veterinarians are good resources because of the sheer volume of feedback they receive about trainers in their area.

If there is a particularly good or bad trainer around, your vet will know.

Other resources for finding dog trainers include your local humane society, pet-supply stores, and the Association of Professional Dog Trainers (APDT) (www.apdt.com).

Bear in mind that dog trainers don't have to be licensed to perform their work. Membership in organizations such as the APDT is a definite plus, but it does not guarantee that a particular trainer is a respectable member of the training community. It is also important to note that the APDT doesn't endorse any of its members. The organization explains on its website that it allows trainers of all methodologies to join in hopes of educating as many people as possible about the importance of humane, science-based training.

If you plan to involve your pup in an organized activity, such as conformation or obedience, it is wise to begin his training with someone who has experience training dogs for this particular pastime. If your goal is simply to teach your puppy good manners, it doesn't matter whether he walks on your left side (the proper place for obedience trials) or right side while on his leash as long as he doesn't pull.

Whether you plan to participate in obedience classes or simply want your puppy to learn the basics of good behavior, your dog's success depends greatly upon the trainer you choose. Although the trainer's role is to show you how to train your dog—not to train him *for* you—the trainer's style and overall tone will become the foundation of your pet's future learning.

Whether you realize it or not, you already have some wonderful resources for finding a great trainer at your disposal.

she should move her body away from your pet so that he is forced to lower his legs to the floor.

At this time, you should use the *sit-stay* command again. Either you or your friend can offer your dog praise for his compliance, but watch your level of enthusiasm. You don't want to sabotage your dog's success by encouraging overexcitement. Solving a jumping problem is about learning to control your dog's overexcitement. Your goal is to keep your pet calm while you welcome guests into your home.

If your dog is so excited that he can't seem to focus on the *sit-stay* position, try using the *down-stay* command instead. He will be less apt to jump from this position. Lying down will also help to keep him calmer in general.

It is essential that your helper give your dog no attention whatsoever until he is sitting or lying down calmly. At this point you may release him from the *stay* command. Ideally, he will then approach your friend with a calmer demeanor. If he jumps up, repeat the above steps, keeping him in the *stay* a bit longer each time. Repeat this exercise as long as your dog seems interested in greeting his guest.

Once he has learned how to greet the guest calmly in this location, move on to another entrance of your home. Even if you only use your front door for accepting packages or pizzas, the delivery personnel will be very grateful that you made the effort to practice your pet's visitor etiquette at this entrance as well. Once your pet has mastered the art of not jumping on people at home, you can move on to bumping into friends in public places, where your dog can also practice his newly acquired good manners.

LEASH PULLING

Even with a dog as small as the Miniature Schnauzer, leash pulling can be an incredibly annoying behavior. In addition to making walks less than leisurely for the owner, this problem behavior has to make the walk less enjoyable for the dog as well. If your dog pulls on his leash, you can solve this common problem with just a few simple steps and some practice.

HOW TO MANAGE IT

If you use a retractable lead with your Miniature Schnauzer, I recommend setting it aside until you have corrected his pulling problem. When it comes to pulling, a leash that extends can make a bad situation worse. A traditional lead will provide your pet with a consistent amount of space to walk within, making it easier for him to understand and accept his boundaries.

Leash pulling can make walks less enjoyable for both owners and dogs.

Also, consider investing in a head harness for your pet instead of a conventional collar. This specially designed harness goes over your Miniature Schnauzer's snout and clasps behind his head. When your dog pulls on his lead while wearing his head harness, he will effectively pull his own head down toward the ground. A dog who can't see where he's going won't pull. (For more advice on managing leash pulling, refer to the "Heel [Walk Nicely on Leash]" section from the previous chapter.)

NIPPING

Some dogs use their teeth when playing with their owners. If this behavior is tolerated when a dog is younger, he may mistakenly think that it is an acceptable thing to do—it isn't. Under no circumstance should you ever allow your dog to place his teeth on your skin.

HOW TO MANAGE IT

Whether he is acting aggressively or just playing, if your dog touches you with his teeth, you must make it clear that this behavior is not acceptable by yelping, "Ouch!" and pulling away, and then not giving your dog further attention. Be sure that everyone else in the household is aware of this rule as well. Kids in particular must understand that even when this kind of behavior seems harmless, it can lead to a dangerous situation down the road.

WHEN TO SEEK PROFESSIONAL HELP

If you think that your dog's problem behavior is more than you can handle alone, reach out for help. Begin by talking to your veterinarian. She may be able to offer you some suggestions that will improve the situation. If you continue to struggle with your pet, it may be time to contact a professional animal behaviorist.

FINDING AN ANIMAL BEHAVIORIST

Animal behaviorists are trainers who work closely with owners and their pets to help eliminate problem behaviors like the ones featured in this chapter. The biggest difference between a conventional dog trainer and a behaviorist is the severity of the problems they address. Whereas most trainers focus on preventing unwanted behaviors and correcting minor problems, behaviorists specialize in solving problems that have become more serious in either frequency or intensity.

Unfortunately, behaviorists do not need to be licensed at this time, so it is very important that you select your behaviorist carefully. The best place to start your search is the Animal Behavior Society (ABS), which certifies individuals in this field. You can find this organization's directory of Certified Applied Animal Behaviorists at www.animalbehaviorsociety.org. Other reliable resources for finding a knowledgeable behaviorist are your veterinarian and your local humane society.

No matter where you find your behaviorist, don't forget to ask for references from her former clients. The educational backgrounds and resumes of behaviorists

can vary, but in general you want someone who has a sound working knowledge of the canine species. Some behaviorists have degrees in psychology or zoology—a definite plus—but never underestimate the value of extensive training experience. Most importantly, you should be comfortable with the person you choose. If you get a bad feeling about a particular behaviorist, keep looking.

If you continue to struggle with your pet, it may be time to contact a professional animal behaviorist.

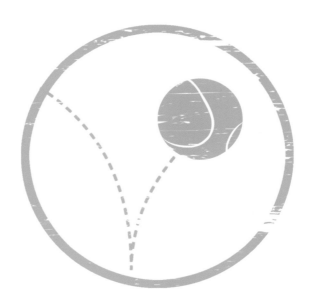

CHAPTER 9

ACTIVITIES WITH YOUR MINIATURE SCHNAUZER

One of the most enjoyable ways to spend time with your Miniature Schnauzer is by participating in organized activities. If you're not much of a joiner, you can involve your dog in your family's activities or in some of your personal hobbies instead. Because this breed is so athletic and intelligent, you have numerous choices of fun pastimes.

AGILITY

One of the more physical canine sports, canine agility is a lot like equestrian jumping competitions. Owners train their pets to navigate complicated obstacle courses consisting of balance beams, chutes, tunnels, and a variety of jumps while being timed. Developed in England in the 1970s, this sport took off in the United States in 1994. One of the things that many owners like best about agility is the amount of owner interaction that is allowed. Owners can cheer as loud as they want for their dogs as they race through the agility course. They can even run alongside them.

Your Miniature Schnauzer must be at least a year old to compete in agility. The reason for this age rule is your dog's safety. Agility can be very strenuous on his body. He will be prone to far fewer injuries once he is 12 months or older.

Agility is a boisterous sport where your dog navigates obstacle courses consisting of ramps, tunnels, and other objects.

Just because your dog cannot compete in agility before the one-year mark doesn't mean that you can't introduce him to the sport. He will probably have an easier time mastering the sport as an adult if he spends some time practicing when he's younger. Just keep him away from activities that pose the biggest threat to his growing bones—such as jumping—until he's older. One of the most challenging parts of agility is getting a dog to run through a chute for the first time, so this task is an excellent starting point for any owner considering this sport.

Beginners to the sport of agility compete in the novice class. The first title your Miniature Schnauzer will earn is that of Novice Agility Dog (NAD). If he continues with the sport, he will then earn his Open Agility Dog (OAD), his Agility Dog Excellent (ADX), and his Master Agility Excellent (MAX), respectively. Each title must be earned through qualifying scores on three different occasions and from two different judges.

CANINE FREESTYLE

Canine freestyle is a relatively new sport headed by the World Canine Freestyle Organization (WCFO). What makes this activity unique is that it provides both you and your pet with an intense workout while allowing you to show off your personalities. Your first choice involves the type of freestyle competition you will enter: musical freestyle or heelwork-to-music. In the former variety, owners and dogs perform original dance routines together. Owners choreograph the routines themselves, and dogs and owners wear matching costumes. In the latter variety, obedience skills are incorporated into the performance.

As with any organized activity, canine freestyle has rules. Judging is done according to a very specific point system, and performing pairs must meet a detailed list of criteria. You can find the 35-page list of these guidelines at the WCFO's website, www.worldcaninefreestyle.org. The best way to decide if you want to try canine freestyle is to attend an event. Many events offer newcomers the opportunity to sign up for a workshop to see if this fun new sport is right for them and their dogs.

CANINE GOOD CITIZEN® TEST

The Canine Good Citizen (CGC) test, sponsored by the American Kennel Club (AKC), was designed to help identify and honor dogs who are the best candidates for activities involving social interaction. This certification is a prerequisite for activities like therapy work, but it is also a useful step if you plan to involve your pet in any organized activity.

The main focus of this ten-step test is obedience, but general good behavior is also considered. How well does your Miniature Schnauzer follow the commands you give him? Does he behave properly in the company of strangers? How about in the middle of a crowd of people? The test even evaluates your pet's

reaction to other dogs and distractions. Passing the CGC test is an impressive accomplishment and one that will open many doors for your dog, quite literally. Dogs who have this certification as part of their resumes are welcome many more places than pets with no such proof of their good behavior.

Because the program encourages responsible pet ownership, you also play a role in your dog's Canine Good Citizen experience. All owners are required to sign the Responsible Dog Owner's Pledge before their dogs take the test. You must promise to care for your pet for the rest of his life and never to allow him to infringe on the rights of others—even to clean up after him in public.

CONFORMATION

The term "canine conformation" is just a fancy way of saying "dog shows." Conformation is one of the oldest organized activities for dogs, and it still draws impressive crowds at the top levels of competition. Only the dogs who match their breed standard most closely usually compete in conformation. While it isn't impossible, it is unlikely that a Miniature Schnauzer who was adopted for his great personality alone will be a serious contender in the show ring.

When it comes to conformation, little things can make a big difference. For example, the Miniature Schnauzer standard states that this breed should have a scissors bite, meaning that the top teeth overlap the bottom teeth in a way that places the inside of the upper incisors just outside the lower incisors when the dog's mouth is closed. A dog with an overshot bite, an undershot bite, or a level bite will be faulted in the ring. Other shortcomings, such as an irregular blaze of white fur on a salt-and-pepper dog, are outright disqualifications. Conformation is essentially an evaluation of breeding stock, so only dogs who have not been spayed or neutered are eligible to participate in these events.

If you select your Miniature Schnauzer carefully and don't mind painstaking grooming, conformation can be a fun pastime. To get started in conformation, I recommend joining your local breed club. These smaller clubs often sponsor single-breed or single-group specialty shows where your dog can get his proverbial feet wet. If your dog does well at the local level, you may even consider traveling with him to compete in larger events.

BE AWARE!

Many canine sports, such as agility and rally, have minimum age requirements, but none of them have maximum age limits. Dogs of any age beyond the minimum requirements can compete in agility, obedience, rally, and even conformation.

Most large shows are all-breed shows. In these events, dogs are divided into seven groups: herding dogs, hounds, non-sporting dogs, sporting dogs, terriers, toys, and working dogs. Dogs are also divided into five classes: puppy, novice, bred by exhibitor, American-bred, and open. Once a dog is judged Best of Breed, he goes on to compete at the group level. The best members from all seven groups compete for the biggest honor, Best in Show.

Only dogs who match their breed most standard closely usually compete in conformation.

Points are awarded for each win, with the specific number depending on the total number of dogs competing and the location of the event. Shows that award three or more points are called "majors." Once a dog has accumulated 15 points or more, he is considered a champion and may use the abbreviation "Ch." before his official name.

EARTHDOG

Because Miniature Schnauzers have such a strong prey instinct, they may do well at earthdog events. This organized activity, also known as "go-to-ground," is a simulated hunting exercise where dogs can demonstrate their highly tuned hunting abilities by chasing prey through tunnels. Only artificial or caged prey is used for these competitions, so no animals are harmed in this process.

Early stages of involvement with this pastime place very little pressure on the dog. Titles aren't even awarded for the Introduction to Quarry (IQ) level. Instead, an owner can see how much potential her pet has for this activity while the dog is given a great opportunity to hone his hunting skills. Dogs who show obvious talent can move on to compete for titles. Your Miniature Schnauzer can earn the title of Junior Earthdog (JE), Senior Earthdog (SE), and even Master Earthdog (ME). Each level is a bit more challenging than the one that preceded it.

One of the best things about earthdog competitions is that the hunt is controlled. By involving your dog in this activity, you provide him with a safe environment to explore his most natural instincts. Earthdog events allow many owners who have no interest in hunting to indulge their pets with absolutely no risk of harming other animals or suffering dangerous bites.

The intelligent, athletic Miniature Schnauzer excels at a variety of dog sports and activities.

OBEDIENCE

If obedience training seems to come easily to your Miniature Schnauzer, he may enjoy competing in formal obedience trials. Some owners find just the word "obedience" a bit intimidating, but this organized activity isn't as oppressive as its name may sound. Most owners and their dogs have a great time competing, and many use it as a springboard for other sports. A dog who does well in obedience may have an easier time following his owner's instructions when it comes to other organized activities.

The introductory level of obedience competition is called the Companion Dog (CD) class. At this stage your dog will need to display a basic understanding of commands. He must heel at different speeds, both on and off his lead. He must also come when called, stay for a certain period of time in the presence of other dogs, and stand while a judge examines him.

The sophomore stage is often called the Open Class, but it is more formally known as the Companion Dog Excellent (CDX) class. The steps involved in this phase include all of the tasks involved in the CD class, but your Miniature Schnauzer will need to perform them off his lead and for longer time periods. Jumping and retrieving tasks are added to this phase of the competition as well for increased difficulty.

If you think that your dog has what it takes to win a Utility Dog (UD) title, he will need to perfect even more difficult tasks, including commands issued with hand signals alone and scent discrimination tasks. The final two tiers of obedience competition are the Obedience Trial Champion (OTCh) and Utility Dog Excellent (UDX). Both of these titles take an enormous amount of time and training, but they are well within the grasp of a well-trained Miniature Schnauzer.

RALLY

If you still think that formal obedience is akin to boot camp, consider rally instead. This activity offers your dog a chance to demonstrate his smarts in a more casual environment. Owners guide their pets through about 10 to 20 stations, where they instruct the dogs to perform different commands. Some stations require the dog to perform an obedience command; others require him

BE AWARE!

If your Miniature Schnauzer seems to be burning out in his organized activity, consider swapping another one, at least temporarily. Sometimes a short break is all a dog needs to come back to a favorite pastime feeling refreshed and passionate about it once again.

to perform an agility-related task. Points are awarded for each station completed. All rally events are also timed, but your dog's time will only come into play in the event of a tie score.

Rally is a fast-paced workout of both the body and the mind. It truly combines athleticism with intellect. Because this activity isn't as physically demanding as straight agility, dogs as young as six months old may compete. Novice rally competitors are allowed to remain on leashes as they navigate the course. The next level of competition, called the Advanced Class, usually involves more stations, which must be completed without a lead, and also includes a jump. The Rally Excellent class increases the number of stations again and features two jumps. To make this level of competition even more challenging, the dog must complete something called the honor exercise: He must remain in a *sit-stay* or *down-stay* for the entire time it takes another dog to complete the rally course.

THERAPY WORK

If your Miniature Schnauzer prefers socialization to sports, therapy work could provide the two of you with a meaningful way to spend your free time.

Therapy dogs visit hospitals and nursing homes with their owners to brighten people's days. Some therapy dogs seem to gravitate toward a particular part of the population—children or the elderly, for instance. If your dog shows such a preference, I highly recommend indulging it. He just may do his best work with this group of people.

Only dogs with the best temperaments are accepted into therapy dog programs. For this reason, one of the best starting points for this pastime is having your dog certified as a Canine Good Citizen. This test is actually a prerequisite for most therapy dog programs. Therapy dogs must also be able to remain at ease in a hospital environment

Therapy dogs visit hospitals, nursing homes, and other locations with their owners to brighten people's days.

among beeping machines, wheelchairs, and occasionally even in the midst of a medical emergency.

If you want to have your Miniature Schnauzer evaluated to see if he would make a good therapy dog, contact Therapy Dogs International (TDI) (www.tdi-dog.org), the largest licensing network for therapy dogs in the world. In addition to passing the Canine Good Citizen test, your dog will need to be cleared by a veterinarian before being allowed to visit patients.

TRAVEL

Traveling can be a tricky issue for pet owners. Leaving your Miniature Schnauzer behind can be hard for both you and your pet, but taking him with you often requires a host of logistics. Will you have to drive instead of fly? Will you be able to find accommodations that allow dogs?

When making your decision, consider the length of your trip and how much time you will be able to spend with your pet. If you will be gone for only a day or two, it may be better to ask a friend to stay with your dog. Leaving him in the care of someone else may also be wise if your travel is business related. Your dog will be much better off with someone who has time to play with him and walk him than he will be in an empty hotel room with no one to keep him company.

If, on the other hand, you are vacationing in the mountains or by the ocean—or visiting family or friends—your dog may enjoy getting away for a while as much as you will.

BY CAR

If you were planning to drive to your destination, your Miniature Schnauzer will likely make an ideal traveling companion. This breed rarely suffers from motion sickness and usually enjoys riding very much. For your pet's safety, it is wise to invest in a canine seat belt attachment for your vehicle. Your dog can also ride safely in his crate, which you can secure with a regular seat belt. Like small children, however, the safest place for your dog is the backseat, due to the dangers associated with automotive airbags.

Be sure to take along plenty of fresh water for your pet for pit stops, and also provide him with the chance to eliminate and stretch his legs during these breaks from riding. I recommend picking up a travel water bowl to take along with you. Another smart idea is to take along items that will entertain your pet during the ride, such as tasty treats or chew toys. Your dog may sleep for a good part of your trip, but if he feels bored, he may be tempted to bark at passing drivers or pedestrians.

If you are planning a vacation and can't imagine leaving your Miniature Schnauzer at home, check into pet-friendly lodging.

BY PLANE

Because many airlines allow small dogs to travel in the plane's cabin with their owners, flying with a Miniature Schnauzer isn't nearly as much of a hassle as traveling by air with a larger pet might be. Do be sure that you get your pet's welcomed status in writing prior to your trip, however. Even airlines that allow canine passengers in the cabin usually have a limit relating to the number of dogs allowed per flight. Also check with the airline to see which health clearances your pet will need, and make sure that you have all this paperwork with you before you head to the airport.

If you will be traveling out of the country, check into the quarantine laws of your destination. As efficient as your airline or travel agent may seem, never rely on information from the person who books your flight—always go straight to the source. The visitor's bureau of your destination should be able to provide you with the most up-to-date information relating to canine travelers. Unless you will be enjoying an extended vacation, however, international travel is usually more of a pain for a pet owner than finding someone trustworthy to look after him while you're gone.

PET-FRIENDLY LODGING

You may be surprised to learn that numerous hotels, motels, and short-term rental housing across the country accept canine guests. I once came across an entire neighborhood of rental homes in Florida near Walt Disney World that allows dogs to stay with their owners. If you are planning a vacation and can't imagine leaving your Miniature Schnauzer at home, check into this growing option. Some establishments charge extra fees for canine guests; others simply ask for a refundable security deposit.

IF YOU CAN'T TAKE YOUR PET WITH YOU

If you opt to travel solo, a professional pet sitter can come to your home to care for your pet when you are away. You can arrange for someone to stop by your house so many times each day to feed your dog and take him for a walk, or you may ask the sitter to stay at your home for the length of your trip.

Your veterinarian should be able to provide you with a list of reliable pet sitters in your area, but interview candidates for this important job carefully nonetheless. Remember, you must trust this individual with both your precious pet and access to your home. Ask for references, be sure to follow up by checking on them, and keep looking if you get a bad feeling about a particular person.

A boarding facility, or kennel, works differently from a pet-sitting service in that you take your dog to the kennel instead of having someone come to your pet. Boarding provides your Miniature Schnauzer with overnight care and should provide him with a certain amount of exercise and playtime during his stay. Choose a kennel with the same scrutiny you would use in selecting a pet sitter. Ask for references, and be sure to tour to the facilities before leaving your pet.

If you utilize the services of a boarding facility, you will need to show proof that your dog is up to date on all his vaccinations prior to his stay. You may even have to ask your veterinarian to give your dog additional shots that the kennel you choose requires. Most vaccines take at least a week to fully protect your pet, so allow yourself plenty of time to make any necessary appointments.

Dog Tale

Just because you have two Miniature Schnauzers doesn't mean that you should expect them to gravitate toward the same organized activities. Whether your dogs were littermates or adopted into your family at different times from different places, they may act a lot like siblings, each preferring his own personal pastime. If one of your dogs enjoys agility and the other likes obedience, you may be able to convince them to compromise on rally. In general, though, it may be good for both dogs to have different areas in which they excel.

RESOURCES

ASSOCIATIONS AND ORGANIZATIONS

BREED CLUBS

American Kennel Club (AKC)
8051 Arco Corporate Drive, Suite 100
Raleigh, NC 27617-3390
Telephone: (919) 233-9767
Fax: (919) 233-3627
E-Mail: info@akc.org
www.akc.org

The American Miniature Schnauzer Club (AMSC)
www.amsc.us

Canadian Kennel Club (CKC)
200 Ronson Drive, Suite 400
Etobicoke, Ontario M9W 5Z9
Telephone: (416) 675-5511
Fax: (416) 675-6506
E-Mail: information@ckc.ca
www.ckc.ca

Fédération Cynologique Internationale (FCI)
FCI Office
Place Albert 1er, 13
B – 6530 Thuin
Belgique
Telephone: +32 71 59.12.38
Fax: +32 71 59.22.29
www.fci.be

The Kennel Club
1-5 Clarges Street, Piccadilly, London W1J 8AB
Telephone: 0844 463 3980
Fax: 020 7518 1028
www.thekennelclub.org.uk

The Miniature Schnauzer Club
www.theminiature
schnauzerclub.co.uk

United Kennel Club (UKC)
100 E. Kilgore Road
Kalamazoo, MI 49002-5584
Telephone: (269) 343-9020
Fax: (269) 343-7037
www.ukcdogs.com

PET SITTERS

National Association of Professional Pet Sitters (NAPPS)
15000 Commerce Parkway, Suite C
Mt. Laurel, New Jersey 08054
Telephone: (856) 439-0324
Fax: (856) 439-0525
E-Mail: napps@petsitters.org
www.petsitters.org

Pet Sitters International
201 East King Street
King, NC 27021-9161
Telephone: (336) 983-9222
Fax: (336) 983-5266
E-Mail: info@petsit.com
www.petsit.com

RESCUE ORGANIZATIONS AND ANIMAL WELFARE GROUPS

American Humane Association
1400 16th Street NW, Suite 360
Washington, DC 20036
Telephone: (800) 227-4645
E-Mail: info@
americanhumane.org
www.americanhumane.org

American Society for the Prevention of Cruelty to Animals (ASPCA)
424 E. 92nd Street
New York, NY 10128-6804
Telephone: (212) 876-7700
www.aspca.org

Royal Society for the Prevention of Cruelty to Animals (RSPCA)
RSPCA Advice Team
Wilberforce Way
Southwater
Horsham
West Sussex
RH13 9RS
United Kingdom
Telephone: 0300 1234 999
www.rspca.org.uk

SPORTS

International Agility Link (IAL)
85 Blackwall Road
Chuwar, Queensland
Australia 4306
Telephone: 61 (07) 3202 2361
Fax: 61 (07) 3281 6872
E-Mail: steve@agilityclick.com
www.agilityclick.com/~ial/

The North American Dog Agility Council (NADAC)
24605 Dodds Rd.
Bend, Oregon 97701
www.nadac.com

North American Flyball Association (NAFA)
1333 West Devon Avenue, #512
Chicago, IL 60660
Telephone: (800) 318-6312
Fax: (800) 318-6312
E-Mail: flyball@flyball.org
www.flyball.org

United States Dog Agility Association (USDAA)
P.O. Box 850955
Richardson, TX 75085
Telephone: (972) 487-2200
Fax: (972) 231-9700
www.usdaa.com

The World Canine Freestyle Organization, Inc.
P.O. Box 350122
Brooklyn, NY 11235
Telephone: (718) 332-8336
Fax: (718) 646-2686
E-Mail: WCFODOGS@aol.com
www.worldcaninefreestyle.org

THERAPY

Pet Partners
875 124th Ave, NE, Suite 101
Bellevue, WA 98005
Telephone: (425) 679-5500
Fax: (425) 679-5539
E-Mail: info@petpartners.org
www.petpartners.org

Therapy Dogs Inc.
P.O. Box 20227
Cheyenne, WY 82003
Telephone: (877) 843-7364
Fax: (307) 638-2079
E-Mail: therapydogsinc@qwestoffice.net
www.therapydogs.com

Therapy Dogs International (TDI)
88 Bartley Road
Flanders, NJ 07836
Telephone: (973) 252-9800
Fax: (973) 252-7171
E-Mail: tdi@gti.net
www.tdi-dog.org

TRAINING

American College of Veterinary Behaviorists (ACVB)
College of Veterinary Medicine, 4474 TAMU
Texas A&M University
College Station, Texas 77843-4474
www.dacvb.org

American Kennel Club Canine Health Foundation, Inc. (CHF)
P. O. Box 900061
Raleigh, NC 27675
Telephone: (888) 682-9696
Fax: (919) 334-4011
www.akcchf.org

Association of Professional Dog Trainers (APDT)
104 South Calhoun Street
Greenville, SC 29601
Telephone: (800) PET-DOGS
Fax: (864) 331-0767
E-Mail: information@apdt.com
www.apdt.com

International Association of Animal Behavior Consultants (IAABC)
565 Callery Road
Cranberry Township, PA 16066
E-Mail: info@iaabc.org
www.iaabc.org

National Association of Dog Obedience Instructors (NADOI)
7910 Picador Drive
Houston, TX 77083-4918
Telephone: (972) 296-1196
E-Mail: info@nadoi.org
www.nadoi.org

VETERINARY AND HEALTH RESOURCES

The Academy of Veterinary Homeopathy (AVH)
P. O. Box 232282
Leucadia, CA 92023-2282
Telephone: (866) 652-1590
Fax: (866) 652-1590
www.theavh.org

American Academy of Veterinary Acupuncture (AAVA)
P.O. Box 1058
Glastonbury, CT 06033
Telephone: (860) 632-9911
www.aava.org

American Animal Hospital Association (AAHA)
12575 W. Bayaud Ave.
Lakewood, CO 80228
Telephone: (303) 986-2800
Fax: (303) 986-1700
E-Mail: info@aahanet.org
www.aahanet.org

American College of Veterinary Internal Medicine (ACVIM)
1997 Wadsworth Blvd.,
Suite A
Lakewood, CO 80214-5293
Telephone: 303-231-9933
Telephone (US or Canada):
(800) 245-9081
Fax: (303) 231-0880
E-Mail: ACVIM@ACVIM.org
www.acvim.org

American College of Veterinary Ophthalmologists (ACVO)
P.O. Box 1311
Meridian, ID 83860
Telephone: (208) 466-7624
Fax: (208) 466-7693
E-Mail: office13@acvo.com
www.acvo.org

American Heartworm Society (AHS)
P.O. Box 8266
Wilmington, DE 19803-8266
E-Mail: info@
heartwormsociety.org
www.heartwormsociety.org

American Holistic Veterinary Medical Association (AHVMA)
P. O. Box 630
Abingdon, MD 21009-0630
Telephone: (410) 569-0795
Fax: (410) 569-2346
E-Mail: office@ahvma.org
www.ahvma.org

American Veterinary Medical Association (AVMA)
1931 North Meacham Road, Suite 100
Schaumburg, IL 60173-4360
Telephone: (800) 248-2862
Fax: (847) 925-1329
www.avma.org

ASPCA Animal Poison Control Center
Telephone: (888) 426-4435
www.aspca.org

British Veterinary Association (BVA)
7 Mansfield Street
London
W1G 9NQ
Telephone: 020 7636 6541
Fax: 020 7908 6349
E-Mail: bvahq@bva.co.uk
www.bva.co.uk

Canine Eye Registration Foundation (CERF)
P.O. Box 199
Rantoul, Il 61866-0199
Telephone: (217) 693-4800
Fax: (217) 693-4801
E-Mail: CERF@vmdb.org
www.vmdb.org

Orthopedic Foundation for Animals (OFA)
2300 E. Nifong Boulevard
Columbia, MO 65201-3806
Telephone: (573) 442-0418
Fax: (573) 875-5073
E-Mail: ofa@offa.org
www.offa.org

US Food and Drug Administration Center for Veterinary Medicine (CVM)
7519 Standish Place
HFV-12
Rockville, MD 20855
Telephone: (240) 276-9300
E-Mail: AskCVM@fda.hhs.gov
www.fda.gov/
AnimalVeterinary/

PUBLICATIONS

BOOKS

Anderson, Teoti. *The Super Simple Guide to Housetraining*. Neptune City: TFH Publications, 2004.

DeGioia, Phyllis. Terra-Nova *The Miniature Schnauzer*. TFH Publications, Inc., 2006.

Moustaki, Nikki. Animal Planet™ *Miniature Schnauzers*. TFH Publications, Inc., 2008.

MAGAZINES

AKC Family Dog
American Kennel Club
260 Madison Avenue
New York, NY 10016
Telephone: (800) 490-5675
E-Mail: familydog@akc.org
www.akc.org/pubs/
familydog

AKC Gazette
American Kennel Club
260 Madison Avenue
New York, NY 10016
www.akc.org/pubs/gazette/
digital_edition.cfm

WEBSITES

Nylabone
www.nylabone.com

TFH Publications, Inc.
www.tfh.com

INDEX

Note: Page numbers in **bold** font indicate a photograph.

PHOTO CREDITS

Allison Herreid (Shutterstock.com): 114
AnnaIA (Shutterstock.com): 4
Budimir Jevtic (Shutterstock.com): 47, 66
dezi (Shutterstock.com): 8, 15, 124, 140
dogist (Shutterstock.com): 17
Elena11 (Shutterstock.com): 79
Elliot Westacott (Shutterstock.com): 40, 107
Eric Isselee (Shutterstock.com): 91
Gina Callaway (Shutterstock.com): 27, 58, 72, 122
gori910 (Shutterstock.com): 26, 60
gorillaimages (Shutterstock.com): 81
Jagodka (Shutterstock.com): back cover, 49, 135, 137
Julia Remezova (Shutterstock.com): 68, 106, 131, 142
katielittle (Shutterstock.com): 37, 95, 101
KPG_Payless (Shutterstock.com): 109
Liliya Kulianionak (Shutterstock.com): 44
Lunja (Shutterstock.com): 74
MaraZe (Shutterstock.com): 6, 7, 36, 67, 90, 96, 98, 102, 127
mariait (Shutterstock.com): 70
Mark Herreid (Shutterstock.com): 120
Maximilian100 (Shutterstock.com): 12, 52, 75
mholka (Shutterstock.com): 56
Mikel Martinez (Shutterstock.com): 116
mitzy (Shutterstock.com): 30, 113
NataSnow (Shutterstock.com): 18
NH (Shutterstock.com): 24
Nikolai Tsvetkov (Shutterstock.com): 1
npine (Shutterstock.com): front cover
Olha Rohulya (Shutterstock.com): 10
Otsphoto (Shutterstock.com): 138
Radule (Shutterstock.com): 20
rebeccaashworth (Shutterstock.com): 31, 129
Rita Kochmarjova (Shutterstock.com): 11, 64
Sergey Lavrentev (Shutterstock.com): 38, 50, 132
Sharon G J Ong (Shutterstock.com): 22, 43

DEDICATION

To Karen Shultz-Stoneburner, who loves animals as much as I do. Kindred spirits make the best friends!

ABOUT THE AUTHOR

Tammy Gagne is a freelance writer who specializes in the health and behavior of companion animals. A two-time Dog Writers Association of America (DWAA) writing competition nominee, she has written more than 100 books for both adults and children. She resides in northern New England with her husband, son, and myriad feathered and furry creatures.

ABOUT ANIMAL PLANET™

Animal Planet™ is the only television network dedicated exclusively to the connection between humans and animals. The network brings people of all ages together by tapping into our fundamental fascination with animals through an array of fresh programming that includes humor, competition, drama, and spectacle from the animal kingdom.

ABOUT *DOGS 101*

The most comprehensive—and most endearing—dog encyclopedia on television, *DOGS 101* spotlights the adorable, the feisty and the unexpected. A wide-ranging rundown of everyone's favorite dog breeds—from the Dalmatian to Xoloitzcuintli —this series surveys a variety of breeds for their behavioral quirks, genetic history, most famous examples and wildest trivia. Learn which dogs are best for urban living and which would be the best fit for your family. Using a mix of animal experts, pop-culture footage and stylized dog photography, *DOGS 101* is an unprecedented look at man's best friend.

At Animal Planet,
we're committed to providing
quality products designed to
help your pets live long,
healthy, and happy lives.